OOPS!

**THE INDISPENSABLE GUIDE
TO RESOLVING YOUR TAX PROBLEM**

OOPS!

THE INDISPENSABLE GUIDE TO RESOLVING YOUR TAX PROBLEM

BENJAMIN P. BUTTERFIELD EA, MBA

Niche Pressworks
Indianapolis, IN

For permission to reprint portions of this content or bulk purchases, contact Ben@BPBTaxResolutions.com.

Author Photograph by: Margaret Wolf Photography
Published by Niche Pressworks; NichePressworks.com
Indianapolis, IN

ISBN
Hardcover: 978-1-962956-37-6
Paperback: 978-1-962956-41-3
eBook: 978-1-962956-38-3

Library of Congress Cataloging-in-Publication Data on File at lccn.loc.gov

To Dad.
Thank you for showing me the importance
of helping others.

Table of Contents

OOPS! is a Must Read for Anyone in Tax Trouble!

When it comes to dealing with tax issues, even the most prepared among us can find ourselves saying, "Oops!" That's why I'm so pleased to introduce *OOPS! The Indispensable Guide to Resolving Your Tax Problem* by Benjamin P. Butterfield. With decades of experience helping clients tackle tax challenges and mentoring other professionals to do the same, I can confidently say that Benjamin has created an amazing resource for anyone navigating the complex world of tax problem resolution.

Benjamin brings a unique blend of expertise and approachability to a topic that often feels intimidating. He understands that tax problems aren't just numbers on a page — they're real-life challenges that can affect every aspect of our lives. Through *OOPS!*, Benjamin offers readers a roadmap that's both practical and reassuring, filled with clear steps, real-world examples, and a touch of humor to lighten the load. This book isn't just a guide; it's like having a trusted friend beside you, helping you face each step with confidence.

What sets *OOPS!* apart is Benjamin's ability to break down complicated concepts into straightforward, actionable advice. He gives you the tools to not only address your immediate tax issues but also to build a foundation of knowledge that will serve you well in the future.

In my own years of experience, I've seen firsthand how empowering it is for clients to understand their options and take proactive steps. *OOPS!* gives you that power, showing you that tax problems are manageable and, in many cases, fixable. By the end of this book, you'll not only have a clear action plan but also the confidence to tackle your tax situation head-on.

So, if you're holding this book, you've already taken a significant step toward resolving your tax concerns. Benjamin Butterfield has crafted a guide that will help you navigate each phase of the journey with clarity and confidence. Here's to transforming "Oops!" moments into resolutions, one step at a time.

Welcome to your first step toward financial peace of mind. You've got this!

With respect and encouragement,
Michael Rozbruch, CPA
Founder, Roz Strategies

CHAPTER 1

Do You Have a Tax Problem?

The best way to teach your kids about taxes
is by eating 30 percent of their ice cream.
— **BILL MURRAY**

Jim looked at the glow of his cell phone sitting on the edge of the light brown nightstand in the master bedroom of their two-story home. 2:12 a.m. Jim and his wife, Beth, went to bed at 10:05 p.m. that night, but as usual, Jim hadn't fallen asleep yet — a common occurrence over the past few months. Glancing at Beth, who was sleeping soundly, Jim thought, *How much longer can I keep my secret from her?*

Was the Internal Revenue Service going to take the house they'd built just five years ago? Would there be a knock at the front door today with special agents carrying Glock 48 pistols ready to take Jim to jail? Could Beth support their two young boys with her meager salary as a kindergarten teacher?

Jim could barely take the pain any longer. *I was just following my dream,* he thought. After working as a professional house painter for ten years, Jim decided he'd had enough working for someone else and opened his own business as a general contractor. Beth had seen how unhappy Jim was and encouraged him to take the plunge into entrepreneurship.

In the beginning, business was booming. Jim had lots of connections from his years working in the painting and home-building industry, which translated into an abundance of work. Before long, he'd hired permanent staff to accompany the handful of subcontractors he already had. Money came in, and life was good!

Six months into his new adventure, Jim drove his new, white Chevy Silverado 1500 to the bank teller business lane window with a big smile on his face. He was about to deposit the biggest check he'd ever seen. This new job was enormous, and his subcontractors were already hard at work, expecting payment for the weeks' time at the site by the end of the day.

"I'm sorry, sir, but this check didn't clear," the bank teller said sternly.

"There must be a mistake," Jim said. "Can you run it through again?"

"No, we cannot. Your client's business account has been frozen. You'll need to contact the payer directly."

Jim went into panic mode. How was he possibly going to pay his workers? He needed cash — and fast. The bank had already loaned him money to start the business, so that wasn't an option. He and Beth had some equity in their home, but Jim didn't want her to think something was wrong; plus, it would take longer than a few hours to access those funds anyway. No-go.

Sitting in his truck in the bank parking lot, Jim considered other possible solutions. "I got it!" he said. "I'll just use the money I set aside to pay taxes, and when this check clears, I'll put the money back!" Problem solved — or so Jim thought.

The workers were paid on time; however, the check never cleared, and Jim had to abandon the big job when the customer went bankrupt. Other customers came in, and business continued, but the money Jim had set aside to pay taxes was gone. *I'll just catch up once the next big customer comes in,* Jim thought. Unfortunately, every time a check came in, the money went right back out to his workers.

Business continued like this for months, and eventually, it was April 15th: Tax Day. Jim knew he wouldn't be able to pay his tax bill, so he filed an extension to get six more months to come up with the money. Customers were coming in, and money was flowing. Certainly he could set aside enough to pay his taxes later that year!

OOPS! Tip: Filing an extension means you've extended time to *file* your taxes. It is not an extension to *pay* your taxes! Any balance owed after April 15th will result in penalties and interest.

Six months came and went. Still, no money saved for taxes. Jim knew he was in a bad situation and waited for the IRS to come knocking. Nothing happened. *Maybe I've slipped through the cracks! After all, I am just a small fry compared to all those millionaires out there,* he thought.

The next year, April 15th came and went, and Jim was so overwhelmed with new business that he barely even thought about filing his taxes. He didn't have money to pay anyway, so why bother? Then, another year flew by. Jim hadn't filed his taxes in three years, and no one made a peep. That is until Jim received a letter from the IRS.

THE DAY OF RECKONING

Jim had dreaded this day. He'd gotten the mail and saw the letter before Beth — thank heaven — and placed it in the glove compartment of his truck to make sure she never saw it. *I'll open it tomorrow,* he thought. That night, Jim was uncharacteristically quiet at the dinner table.

"Is everything okay?" Beth asked with concern.

"Oh, yeah, of course. Just a long day at work," Jim replied.

The next morning, after Beth left to take the kids to school and head to work, Jim went out to his truck. Looking at the letter, Jim tore it open with sweaty palms and shaky hands. He felt lightheaded. After reading a few lines, he dropped the letter and began to sob.

The IRS letter lay face up on the floor of Jim's Chevy. In bold font across the top of the page it said, "Please pay $123,785 within the next 30 days."

I'm in a real mess, Jim thought. *There is no way I can come up with this kind of cash. How is it possible to owe the IRS anything since I didn't even file my tax returns?*

OOPS! Tip: The IRS can file your tax return without your permission! This is called a substitute for return (SFR) and is quite common when you don't file your taxes but a third party reports income you've made from them directly to the IRS.

Not knowing what to do, Jim decided to remain blissfully ignorant and pretend nothing had happened. Weeks went by, then months. Multiple letters arrived from the IRS, but Jim just threw them in the glove compartment of this truck. After all, since he hadn't filed his tax returns, did he really owe the money? Not willing to acknowledge his actions, Jim tried to justify his ignorance.

One day, there was a note in his mailbox saying Jim had a certified letter from the IRS waiting for him at the post office. Nervously, Jim drove down the street and retrieved the letter, putting it in his glove compartment, unopened, with the others. This one, however, bothered him. It looked different than the previous letters, more serious. It was thicker and had a green certified mail sticker on it.

And now, here Jim was, laying sleepless in bed.

The next day, Beth came home from work with a head full of steam. "Jim!" she yelled as she stepped through the front door. Jim had gotten home first, something he'd been doing lately to intercept any more IRS letters. "The Human Resources department at work just gave me a letter saying the State was going to take eighty percent of my next paycheck! Do you know anything about this?"

OOPS! Tip: Don't forget about *State* income tax! States tend to be even more aggressive than the IRS. And yes, the State can force your employer to withhold a very large percentage of your future paychecks (yep, plural!) to pay down your tax liability. This is called a wage garnishment and is very difficult to undo once it's started.

The jig was up. Jim sat down, put his head on the kitchen table, and cried like he'd never cried before. Beth put her arm around his shoulders. "Whatever it is, it will be okay. We'll figure it out together," Beth said with a trembling voice.

Jim walked out to his truck, opened the glove compartment stuffed full of letters from the IRS, gathered up the papers, walked back into the house, and dumped the letters on the kitchen table. He told Beth everything, from the big job that went south to not filing tax returns. Jim's voice was shaking, something Beth had never heard before. He finally caught her gaze. Beth looked shocked, frightened, and pale. "I need to get some air," Beth said quietly as she slowly stood up and nervously walked outside.

How could I let this happen? Beth wondered. *Jim has always been responsible with bills. I just assumed he'd filed our tax returns on time. I'm so naïve.* Beth's job as a teacher caused plenty of stress as it was, and the demands of being the mom of two active boys had her running all over town. Now this? Beth felt totally defeated.

As Beth walked around the well-manicured, suburban neighborhood, she felt overcome with anxiety. "What if we lose the house? What would the neighbors say if they saw us being kicked out? Would the boys have to switch schools?" she wondered aloud. This was just too much for her to handle right now.

Beth stopped walking, gathered herself, and took three deep breaths. "No," she said. "We've been through tough times before, and we can make it through this. There must be a way out!" Walking back to the house with a spring in her step, Beth muttered, "We are good people. We don't hurt anyone; we volunteer our time and are raising good kids. I'm sure there are others in this situation who found a solution."

Beth opened the front door and saw Jim walking in circles around the kitchen. Walking to their shared workspace, she sat down at the computer and immediately started looking for a solution online. It didn't take long for her to stumble across an article that said, "The IRS has a Fresh Start Initiative. You can settle your tax debt for pennies on the dollar with a program called offer in compromise (OIC)."

"Bingo!" Beth exclaimed. After digging into the process of submitting an offer and all the documents that were required, Beth was back to being overwhelmed. "We need someone to help us," she told Jim.

THE SEARCH FOR HELP

Not knowing exactly who to contact, Jim called several local CPA firms and got the same response each time: "You're in a real mess; this is a more complex situation than we can handle. You need to find someone who specializes in tax resolution." Naturally, Beth googled "Tax Resolution" and found dozens of organizations.

"Which one should we choose?" Jim asked.

"Just start calling them," Beth responded.

The first company looked promising. It had a nice website, bold promises, and a quick turnaround. After twenty seconds of ringing, there was no answer, and there was no way Jim was going to leave a voicemail with his personal tax information.

On to the next company.

Phone number disconnected.

Bummer.

He tried another company. *Finally, a human!* Jim had barely provided any information before the guy promised he could get Jim and Beth's IRS balance down to zero dollars with the OIC program. All he needed was a twenty-thousand-dollar down payment.

How can this guy possibly get the balance that low without knowing the details of our situation? Jim wondered. *No thanks.*

Frustrated, Jim threw his hands up in the air in defeat. "Isn't there anyone credible out there?" he yelled.

"How about we look at the Better Business Bureau?" Beth responded. Filtering their search to only view the A+ rated tax resolution firms certainly narrowed the results, but there were still a small handful of companies listed. After looking at the Google Reviews for all these companies, Beth gasped and said, "Look, Jim, this one has so many amazing reviews! Call them now!"

My phone rang.

HELP HAS ARRIVED

Jim was a nervous mess. I could tell he was embarrassed to share his story, and he was barely able to get the words out as he spoke. After a few sentences, I stopped him.

"Jim, it's okay," I said. "I've been helping people resolve their tax issues for many years and have seen it all. There is absolutely no judgment on my part. The only way we are going to slay this dragon is if we can see him. Be honest with me so I can get you protected."

Jim let out a deep sigh. "I don't want to lose my house or go to jail. Is that something you can help with?" he asked.

"While those situations are rare, they do happen," I said. "Let me ask you a few more questions to see if we're a good fit for you."

OOPS! Tip: Is jail time possible? Just ask the dentist in Connecticut who was sentenced to ten months in prison for tax evasion, the rehab manager in Florida who was sentenced to three years in prison for tax evasion and other crimes, or the two former New York police officers who started a security business, failed to pay taxes, and were sentenced to six months in prison. You bet it's possible!

After going through some brief questions, I asked, "Jim, are you ready to fix this tax problem now?"

"Yes, we are!" he said.

"Okay, I just want to make sure you are fully committed to this process. It's going to take a while, but I'm confident we can help you."

Clearly relieved, Jim said, "Thank you so much! We've read about a program called offer in compromise, where the IRS will settle our tax debt for less than what we owe. Can we do that program?"

"Jim, OIC is an excellent program the IRS offers and is one of the first things we look at in situations like this. Unfortunately, you don't qualify due to all the equity in your home. But fear not, we are going to set up an installment agreement with the IRS that will also save you lots of money."

OOPS! Tip: Be careful! Many tax resolution firms will push you into submitting an OIC to the IRS after paying the firm a boatload of money just to end up having your offer denied because you didn't really qualify in the first place. In fact, as a part of the IRS's list of Dirty Dozen tax scams, they warn taxpayers of these "OIC mills" that aggressively mislead taxpayers into thinking their tax debts can just disappear.

THE OOPS! PROCESS

The next step was to begin walking Jim through our OOPS! process for resolving tax problems. "Okay, Jim," I said. "First, we need to organize your records. Bring me all the letters you received, your company's books, and any other tax documents from the three years when you didn't pay taxes. I'll also give you a tax organizer list to make sure we have everything."

"Uh, what do you mean by *company's books*?" Jim asked.

"You know, records of the amount of money you made and all of the business expenses you have," I responded.

"What if I don't have books?" Jim said.

"No worries," I told him. "We'll create them for you."

Shifting topic, I said, "The second step is to observe the tax laws and get compliant. This means we are going to file your back tax returns."

"Okay, that sounds easy enough. What do you need from me?" Jim asked.

"I'll be reaching out to you directly throughout this entire process. Just respond to my questions as quickly as possible so we can keep things moving forward. Remember, I am here to protect you. I will take care of all the details. You just need to get me what I ask for," I said.

"Third, we will patch up the damage that was done. For you, Jim, that means getting an installment agreement with the Internal Revenue Service in place so there is no further threat of aggressive collection activity. Also, I'll contact the state's Department of Revenue to see if there's anything I can do about the wage garnishment coming up on Beth's paycheck."

"Okay," Jim said. "This sounds like the step that fixes everything, right?"

"Exactly!" I told him. "Finally, the fourth step is to safeguard your assets against future problems. Here, we'll discuss things you can put in place, so this problem doesn't happen again."

"This sounds like something I should have done in the beginning, right?" Jim responded.

"That's right, Jim. The good news is that we can start this now and look forward to brighter days!"

WHAT THIS BOOK CAN DO FOR YOU

You're likely a good person trying to do the right thing, and somehow, you've found yourself a bit sideways with the IRS or your State, and you're not sure what to do about it. And, like Jim and Beth, once you're ready to resolve the issue, it feels impossible to sift through all the available information, identify credible and accurate resources, interpret complicated tax language, and know which tax professionals you can trust.

Let me help you with that.

I've been aiding taxpayers for more than ten years and saved millions of dollars for my clients. I'm an Enrolled Agent, have an MBA, and became a Certified Tax Resolution Specialist. I am the founder of BPB Tax Resolutions, an A+ Better Business Bureau-rated company dedicated to fixing tax problems for people like you.

Throughout *OOPS!: The Indispensable Guide to Resolving Your Tax Problem* I am going to explain the steps you can take to survive the pressure the IRS is putting on you. I'll walk you through my OOPS! process in detail so you have the knowledge to resolve your tax dilemma once and for all.

It's going to be okay, my friend. Read on.

CHAPTER 2

Taxes... And Lawn Fertilizer?

*Ikea has been accused of failing to pay
$500 million in taxes. But prosecutors are having
a hard time putting their case together.*

I haven't always been in the tax resolution business. Armed with an accounting degree and a head full of hopes and dreams, I secured a job in the finance department of a large corporation, where I worked hard and accumulated experience in many different areas of finance and accounting. Eventually, I became a Certified Management Accountant and got my MBA from the University of Nebraska.

While going through the MBA program, I took a business law course. The professor was amazing, and although the class was hard, I loved it! Reviewing cases, preparing for arguments, and presenting alternative solutions — so much work and stress, yet at the same time, so enjoyable to me. The professor allowed us to defend our test answers in front of the class to potentially earn points back — my favorite part!

The next semester I had a class in taxation. I really didn't like preparing tax returns, other than writing numbers in those neat little boxes (yes, this occurred before the internet was mainstream); however, I did have a way with numbers, and the convergence of solving problems, defending a position, and helping people clicked in my brain. I knew that at some point, I'd find a way to use this unique set of skills.

Life happened, as it usually does, and I got busy with my career and raising three amazing kids. Soccer, flag football, basketball, marching band, theater; you name it, I was involved. And usually not as a spectator. I loved to coach! Working with those kids was a real treat for me. Watching them grow and improve was so rewarding. At that time in my life, I knew I was where I needed to be.

Eventually, the nagging bug I had for taxes and law started to become a burning desire. I studied for and passed the exam to become an Enrolled Agent.

OOPS! Tip: An Enrolled Agent is a federally authorized tax practitioner empowered directly by the US Department of the Treasury. Enrolled Agents represent taxpayers before the IRS for tax issues like audits, collections, and appeals. It is the highest credential awarded by the IRS.

"Well, now what?" I asked myself. I decided to start preparing tax returns for more than just friends and family during the evenings and weekends and created a company I named BPB Tax Services — the first iteration of what is now BPB Tax Resolutions. Before long, I'd secured a handful of clients and was officially a small business owner!

It didn't take long for a client to come to me with a real problem. He hadn't filed taxes in several years and now the IRS had filed a substitute for return (SFR) for him (remember those from the first chapter?). Not having tackled this type of situation before, I bungled my way through calling the IRS multiple times, meeting with the taxpayer, gathering information, and repeating the process all over again. Eventually, I got his original taxes filed and saved him thousands in penalties and interest.

This was so much more satisfying to me than just churning away at preparing tax returns! I did some research and found myself an amazing mentor. From that point on, I was a sponge. I completed tons of training to learn the art of tax problem resolution. I helped more and more people and had great success. However, my process was inefficient and not always easy to explain to my clients. I knew there had to be a better way.

LIGHTNING STRIKES

Like a bolt of lightning, it occurred to me that I needed to design a process like my yard guy! What does a yard have to do with tax problem resolution, you ask? Let me explain.

When we were raising a young family, we purchased a lovely house in the suburbs. It was perfect for us! Good space inside, a large kitchen and dinette, and a beautiful yard with lush green grass. Oh, to feel the full-bodied Kentucky bluegrass under your bare feet while running through the sprinkler on a hot summer day in Nebraska! I was dead set on maintaining that gorgeous lawn all by myself. So, I did what every other suburban homeowner did during the summer: I went to the hardware store.

I didn't know exactly what I was doing, but I was smart (after all, I had an MBA, right?), wanted to save money, and was confident I could figure it out. I walked to the outdoor section and immediately spotted the yard chemicals where I saw a bag that said, "Lawn Food and Fertilizer, Apply in Summer." Bingo! I bought a bag, a rotary fertilizer spreader, and a pack of gum.

I woke up early the next morning, excited to give my picturesque yard a treat. Setting the spreader on the grass I started to open the bag of yard food and noticed it said, "Step 3." Of course, I ignored the label, thinking there wouldn't be any problem because, after all, the description said to use the product in the summer, and it was June.

I'd studied physics in high school like everyone else, but evidently, I'd forgotten all the principles and haphazardly cut a large hole in the bag with my handy utility knife. The hole I'd cut was too big, and while pouring the chemicals into the spreader, the bag slipped and dropped into one side of the spreader, causing the unit to fall over and dump the fertilizer into one big pile in the grass. "Nuts!" I exclaimed. "This is probably not good."

I pulled the spreader upright and started putting the spilled lawn food back into the bag with our dog's pooper-scooper, a small garden shovel, and my hands. When it looked like I'd returned most of the fertilizer back into the bag, I got to work. I figured the patch of grass that I spilled on would just be a little happier than the rest of the yard.

Grinning from ear to ear, I walked around the yard in even lines, spreading love on all my little blades of grass. "This is easy!" I bellowed. Sure, now and again, the wheel of the spreader would fall into some sort of gopher hole and dump a little extra in the area, but I had no worries!

After applying yard food to my entire lawn, I put the spreader away, grabbed an iced tea, and sat on the deck. Ah, the joy of being a do-it-yourself homeowner! I was so proud and couldn't wait to see the beautiful fruits of my labor.

I watered the grass regularly, mowed and trimmed, and basked in the glory of my success. Until I saw patches of grass turning brown. How could this be? I pretty much followed the instructions on the bag. Shouldn't my lawn be happy? Most of the grass was nice and green, but there were obvious spots of dead grass that looked wonky. And the area where I spilled the fertilizer in the beginning? Totally dead.

Disappointed, I went back to the hardware store, bought some grass seed, threw it on the brown patches, and watered the heck out of it. After several weeks, there were no new grass blades. Talk about scorched earth! Over the next few weeks, I kept mowing, trimming, watering, and pulling up weeds.

In time, the weeds became too plentiful to pull one by one, so I decided it was time for some weed killer. I went back to the hardware store, found some weed killer that also contained lawn food, returned home, and *carefully* applied it with my spreader. The bag was labeled "Step 2," but hey, I needed to kill these weeds, and fast! After a few days, some of the weeds withered up a little and I pulled up any remaining weeds that didn't die from the fertilizer.

Fall came, and I watered and mowed for the last time, winterized my equipment, and let the cold, Midwest winter come and go. Soon, spring was upon us, and I was excited to get back to caring for my beautiful yard. Except, it wasn't so beautiful. The grass looked horrible. It was covered in brown spots, weeds, and uneven patches of grass.

Okay, no problem, I thought. I'd learned my lesson and was going to make this year's yard better.

I did some research and was determined to whip this yard back into shape. I missed the window for the first application again, but I applied Step 2 and Step 3 in perfect order and exactly as the instructions said. Winter arrived quickly that year, so I missed the fourth and final step, but at least I'd gotten the timing of the second and third applications right!

The following spring, my grass looked even worse, and I finally realized I needed help from someone who knew what they were doing, so I called a professional yard service.

A week later, the yard guy met me at my house, looked around the yard, and smiled before saying, "You tried to do this on your own, didn't you?"

"Uh, yes," I said sheepishly.

"Well, Mr. Butterfield, this is going to take some time. It will probably be three or four years before I get your lawn looking amazing," he said.

"That long? Really?" I asked.

"Yes, really. I have a proven process for success. You just need to trust in me and this process. Can you do that?"

I didn't have much of a choice. My yard was already the butt of neighborhood jokes. "What's the process?" I questioned.

"First, we need to organize a plan for the year — or, in your case, the next few years — and prepare the yard. We do this by aerating and laying down crabgrass preventer to allow for healthy grass to grow," he explained.

"I've never heard of aerating. What is that?" I asked.

"It's a step that prepares the yard by creating holes in the soil so nutrients and water can get down to the roots," he said.

Geez, I never knew aerating was even an option! I thought. *Thank heavens I called a professional.*

"Then," he continued, "we need to obey the rules of nature by applying lawn food to nourish the grass and weed control to kill the dandelions long before they get to the puffball stage. This is done in late spring. After that, we'll patch up the grass by overseeding once or twice during the summer."

I was impressed. I really appreciated how this guy was taking the time to explain the process to me.

"Finally, we'll safeguard and protect the grass in the fall by laying down some more lawn food. This will build strong, deep, and healthy roots for a better lawn in the spring," he said.

"Is there anything I need to do?" I asked.

"Mow the grass once a week and water three times a week during the summer, cut it down to twice a week in the early fall. *Don't do anything else,*" he stressed. "If you follow the steps — organize, obey, patch, and safeguard — we can get your yard looking and feeling the way you want."

Knowing what he meant, I grunted.

Fast forward three years, and my yard was the envy of the neighborhood! People asked me what I'd done to create such a work of art. "I hired a professional instead of trying to do this on my own," I responded.

THE OOPS! PROCESS IS BORN

The process my yard guy followed was simple yet proven and effective. This was the solution I'd been searching for! I needed to design a process for helping my clients just like my yard guy had a process for helping homeowners! The steps were very similar; I just needed to reframe the experience to apply to tax resolution.

Instead of organizing a plan for the yard, I taught my clients to organize their records when we started helping them. As an alternative to observing the laws of nature, we had to observe the tax laws and get compliant. Third, we needed to patch up the damage that was done, not to the grass but to the taxpayer's IRS standing. Finally, instead of safeguarding against the upcoming winter, I had to coach my clients to safeguard against future tax problems. "Yahtzee!" I exclaimed. "My clients just need to fix their OOPS!"

OOPS! Tip:
Here are the four steps to tax problem resolution.

1. **O**rganize your records.
2. **O**bserve the tax laws and get compliant.
3. **P**atch up the damage that was done.
4. **S**afeguard against future tax problems.

If you're struggling to tackle your tax issues by yourself, I understand how you feel. As you can see, I also needed someone to help me in a time of need. They gave me a process to follow, I trusted that process, and we achieved successful results. In the next few chapters, I'm going to give you a step-by-step breakdown of the OOPS! process so you can achieve the results you want and the peace of mind that you crave and deserve.

CHAPTER 3

You Have Rights as a Taxpayer!

*You must pay taxes. But there's no law
that says you gotta leave a tip.*
— MORGAN STANLEY

Bob was a client of mine who came to me with his hands thrown up in the air. "I give up!" he exclaimed. "I'm tired of dealing with the IRS. Can you help me?"

"Well, Bob," I said, "let's go through a few details to see if we're a good fit for each other."

Bob jumped right in. "I received a letter in the mail from the IRS claiming that I owe them $23,000. I own a small business, and we file and pay all our taxes on time. I have no idea what the bill is for. The letter stated that if I disagreed with the assessment, I should send them a letter explaining why."

"So, that's what I did," he continued. "I made the letter clear and simple, asking for a more detailed explanation of what this balance was related to. A month later, I received another letter from the IRS saying they needed an additional 60 days to respond. The letter also said that if I wanted to just pay the balance off in the meantime, I could simply write a check payable to the United States Treasury and include my name, address, employer identification number, the tax year, and the tax form associated with the payment."

"I saw that and thought, *What? Pay it off? I don't even know what this is for*," Bob said. "Why would I pay for something I don't owe?"

Bob told me he'd decided to wait 60 days for the IRS to respond and at about the 60-day mark, he received another letter from the IRS that looked just like the first one but with a different date. This second letter asked for an additional 60 days. Also, the balance shown on the letter was even higher than the first! Upon further investigation, Bob realized the amount of interest and penalties had increased.

"It was like a snowball rolling down a hill," Bob exclaimed. "The IRS was charging *me* because *they* needed more time! I decided enough was enough and called the IRS directly," Bob said.

Bob explained that he'd called the toll-free phone number listed in the IRS letter. "I'm surprised they didn't charge me for the phone call," Bob said sarcastically. After a few rings, he'd been greeted by hold music — of course — and a message thanking him for his patience and telling him that the wait time would be more than an hour. After waiting on hold for more than two hours, the call got disconnected.

Clearly frustrated, Bob told me what happened next. "I called back the next day and waited nearly three hours before I finally talked to someone. They were very difficult to understand, and they asked for all kinds of information. I just wanted to know what the bill was for! The agent kept pressuring me to pay the amount due or set up payments. I couldn't convince them that the amount listed was not my balance! The call lasted more than an hour, and I got nowhere, so I hung up."

Bob took a deep breath and continued. "A week later, I called again. This time, I was on hold for *only* ninety minutes. The agent answered, and I had to explain my entire situation all over again. Throughout the conversation, the IRS agent kept telling me they needed to research my file, and they asked to put me on a five to seven-minute hold while they did. What was I going to say? No? This cycle happened at least four times."

"Anyway, each time they came back to the call, they had more questions than answers," Bob said with a sigh. "Don't these guys know the tax laws? I thought they were there to help me understand why I received this letter! Eventually — even though they didn't fully know why the letter was sent —the agent told me that this balance wasn't going away and the only way to get rid of it was to pay in full or set up payments with them. I felt like I was talking to a bill collector and not someone there to help!"

> **OOPS! Tip:** The IRS is not set up to fight *for* you. Most of the time, when you call the IRS, you're calling the Collections Division, and their job is to — wait for it — collect money. You need to be your own advocate!

YOU HAVE RIGHTS!

After carefully listening to Bob's situation, I told him I thought I could be of some help. Bob was understandably upset because he felt like the IRS was out to get him. While Bob's scenario is different than Beth and Jim's, there is an important commonality I'd like to go through with you: The Taxpayer Bill of Rights.

Also known as Publication 1, The Taxpayer Bill of Rights explains your rights as a taxpayer and the processes for examination, appeal, collection, and refunds.[1] The ten rights you're entitled to as a taxpayer are as follows:

---

1 "Taxpayer Bill of Rights: The Ten Rights of Every Taxpayer." Internal Revenue Service, September 11, 2024. https://www.irs.gov/newsroom/taxpayer-bill-of-rights-the-ten-rights-of-every-taxpayer.

1. **The Right to Be Informed.** Taxpayers have the right to know what they need to do to comply with tax laws and what decisions the IRS made regarding their tax account.

2. **The Right to Quality Service.** Taxpayers have the right to receive clear and understandable assistance from the IRS and to speak to a supervisor about inadequate service.

3. **The Right to Pay No More than the Correct Amount of Tax.** Taxpayers have the right to pay only the amount of tax legally due.

4. **The Right to Challenge the IRS's Position and Be Heard.** Taxpayers have the right to raise objections in response to formal IRS actions or proposed actions and can expect the IRS to reply.

5. **The Right to Appeal an IRS Decision in an Independent Forum.** Taxpayers are entitled to a fair and impartial administrative appeal of most IRS decisions.

6. **The Right to Finality.** Taxpayers have the right to know the maximum amount of time they have to challenge an IRS position and the amount of time the IRS has to audit a particular tax year and collect a tax debt.

7. **The Right to Privacy.** Taxpayers have the right to expect that any IRS inquiry, examination, or enforcement action will be no more intrusive than necessary.

8. **The Right to Confidentiality.** Taxpayers have the right to expect that any information they provide to the IRS will not be disclosed unless authorized by the taxpayer or law.

9. **The Right to Retain Representation.** Taxpayers have the right to retain an authorized representative of their choice to represent them in their dealings with the IRS.

10. **The Right to a Fair and Just Tax System.** Taxpayers have the right to expect the tax system to consider facts and circumstances that might affect their underlying liabilities, ability to pay, or ability to provide information timely.

While some of the rights were laughable to Bob (like The Right to Quality Service), the IRS is bound to act in accordance with these regulations, and I believe it does the best it can to uphold them. Still, it is important for you to know *you do have rights!* Be confident and know that these rights are in place to protect you from poorly trained IRS employees.

Before we got started, I first discussed Right #3 with Bob: The Right to Pay No More than the Correct Amount of Tax. Knowing that the amount of tax the IRS claimed he owed was incorrect gave Bob immediate relief.

Next, I told him about Right #4: The Right to Challenge the IRS's Position and Be Heard. Taxpayers have the right to raise objections in response to formal IRS actions (or proposed actions). "This is exactly what we are going to do, Bob," I said. "Basically, we're going to tell them 'No,' and have *them* prove that you are responsible for this liability."

"What if we talk to an IRS agent who's just having a bad day and doesn't listen to us?" Bob asked.

"Ah, that is where Right #5 comes into play!" I said. "The Right to Appeal an IRS Decision in an Independent Forum." I explained that being heard in Appeals happens all the time, and we could often get great results in Appeals. Bob was relieved when I said this.

Bob had one other major concern. He was afraid to give the IRS any additional information as he owned a business and believed that if his customers found out about this IRS *issue*, they would leave him.

"You led me directly to Right #8: The Right to Confidentiality," I explained. "Any information you give the IRS will not be disclosed unless you authorize it or if required by law. There are stiff penalties for those who wrongfully use or disclose taxpayer return information."

"Okay, Ben, you've convinced me that you know what you're talking about. What's next?" Bob asked.

"Taxpayer Right #9, of course!" I responded.

"What's that?" Bob asked.

"Your Right to Retain Representation!" I said with a smile.

OOPS! Tip: When you retain someone to help you with your tax problem, they'll file one of two forms (or both), and it's critical that you understand the difference between the two. The first is a *Form 8821 Tax Information Authorization.* This enables the professional to obtain your confidential tax information verbally or in writing. The second is *Form 2848 Power of Attorney,* which can only be filed by a professional eligible to practice before the IRS. Form 2848 is more powerful and authorizes the professional to represent you and take action on your behalf. If a tax professional tells you they're working with the IRS on your behalf, but you never signed a Form 2848, that professional is not telling you the truth!

Now, it was time to take Bob through the OOPS! process to Organize, Obey, Patch, and Safeguard his assets. First, Bob and I worked together for a few weeks to organize his documentation before I called the IRS. He was already obeying the tax laws, as all required returns were filed and paid, so we just had to patch things up with the IRS. Bob already had adequate safeguards in place to ensure he stayed compliant in future years.

My call with the IRS didn't initially bear any fruit. However, I fight vigorously for the clients I represent and kept digging and digging, not letting the agent off the hook even though it sounded like they didn't really want to be there. After some healthy conversation, we discovered an SFR (there's that acronym again!) had been filed by the IRS for Bob based on some internal systematic trigger.

Bam! I knew exactly what had to be done. We had to file a zero return with the IRS Service Center to get that SFR replaced. I prepared the return, contacted Bob to let him know what we were doing, and then sent the return to the IRS.

OOPS! Tip: When replacing a substitute for return, you need to file an *original* return, *not* an amended return! If you didn't have any income, then you'd file a zero return (a return with zero dollars as the income).

After a few weeks of waiting for the IRS to process the zero return I'd submitted, the results came back, and I got to make my favorite phone call. "Bob, I have good news!" I said. "I was able to get your entire $23,000 balance wiped out to zero!"

If you're in a similar situation, it's important to know that you have rights. The IRS can't just come after you willy-nilly. When you are talking with an IRS agent, remember Rule #10 from The Taxpayer Bill of Rights and be confident that you have the right to a fair and just tax system.

CHAPTER 4

Stop Hiding

We'll try to cooperate fully with the IRS, because, as citizens, we feel a strong patriotic duty not to go to jail.
— DAVE BARRY

Oftentimes, my clients will ask, "Am I going to go to jail?"

My answer is usually, "It's highly unlikely, but possible. I'm here to try to prevent that." The case does have to be relatively extreme for jail time to be on the table, but the federal government has quite a bit of power here, and you don't want to tempt it.

Thankfully, after working with hundreds of clients, not one person under my protection has gone to prison. And I don't plan on that changing anytime soon. I inform my clients that if they are honest with me and do what I say when I say to do it, jail should never happen.

Still, jail time *is* possible. As you'll see in the next few paragraphs, people do go to jail for shirking their tax obligations. Let these stories be a warning to you.

PRISON CAN HAPPEN

Have you ever heard of Al Capone? Capone was born in Brooklyn, New York, in January 1899 and started life as a gangster when he quit school after the sixth grade. Around 1920, Capone was invited to join the notorious Colosimo mob in Chicago.[2]

Back in those days, the Prohibition Amendment made the manufacture and sale of alcohol illegal, but not the consumption or private possession of it. A huge opportunity to brew and sell alcohol was created, and Capone took full advantage of it, making him very wealthy before his 30th birthday.

Capone quickly became the biggest mob boss in Chicago and ran numerous racketeering activities in the late 1920s. The FBI spent years trying to take him down, but Capone's legitimate businesses, influence over public officials, and connection with labor unions helped shield him.

Capone's lavish lifestyle, expensive suits, glimmering jewelry, and stays at the best hotels made

---

2 "Al Capone." Federal Bureau of Investigation, May 18, 2016. https://www.fbi.gov/history/famous-cases/al-capone.

agents in the federal government wonder, *How could a guy with all these niceties of life claim to not have any taxable income?*

After years of investigation, the federal authorities had a breakthrough. While they couldn't prove charges for crimes related to all the murders and racketeering endeavors, they could get him on something. What was it? Tax evasion! Believe it or not, Capone, one of the most famous mob bosses of all time, who was able to duck and dodge the FBI for years, got caught by the IRS! Crazy, right?

The tax evasion charge almost didn't hold up since Capone had bribed the whole jury to rule in his favor. Fortunately, the judge found out, switched juries with a courtroom down the hall, and sequestered the new jurors so Capone's posse couldn't get to them. Eventually, Al Capone was found guilty and sentenced to eleven years in Alcatraz for failing to file his tax returns!

I understand this is an extreme example; however, it just had to be said. There was no way I was going to leave a story as fascinating as this out of a chapter about the power of the federal government when it comes to taxes.

Looking for a more recent story? How about the man from Ohio who ran a small family business removing worn-out railroad track to sell to scrap metal companies? This guy filed false tax returns from 2013 to 2016 and was sentenced to twelve months in prison.

Or perhaps the Chicago businessman who was sentenced to two years in prison for tax evasion from 2010 to 2013? He ran a security company and, among other crimes, used his business to pay for many personal services that were later classified as business expenses.

There was also a temp agency owner who was convicted of mail fraud and for failing to pay payroll taxes. She paid her employees with a combination of cash and checks and was able to hide her total payroll balance, which allowed her to avoid paying a significant amount of payroll taxes. She faces up to twenty-five years in prison.

The list goes on and on. The point is this: *stop hiding!* All these stories are about regular people who were hiding from their obligation to file and pay their taxes. Don't let this be you!

WHAT ABOUT MY STUFF?

Another common question I'm asked is, "Will the IRS take my house?" This is also an instance where the outcome is unlikely but possible. The government isn't in the business of making people homeless, so the circumstances must be dire before the IRS takes possession of and sells a home to recover their money.

However, it *is* very common for the IRS to file a public document called a Notice of Federal Tax Lien to protect their interests. This alerts creditors that the government has a legal right to your property.

> **OOPS! Tip:** *Liens* and *levies* are different. A lien is a legal claim against your property, whereas a levy allows the government to take your property. They often happen sequentially, with the lien happening first before the situation is escalated into a levy.

A lien is often misinterpreted as only pertaining to your house. However, it's attached to *all* your assets! Cars, boats, property, securities, etc. are all fair game. It also doesn't just apply to the things you currently own but also to things you buy in the future until your tax debt is paid. Read that again. Once the IRS files a lien, it sticks to all your current and future assets like glue! Needless to say, this is not ideal. A federal tax lien can wreak havoc on your life.

One day, I received a panicked call from a taxpayer who'd sold her house and was planning to use the proceeds to purchase another house. One week before closing, the title company called and told her there was a problem. The IRS had an active lien on her property in the amount of $65,000. The proceeds from the sale of her house weren't enough to pay off the lien *and* purchase the new home. Yikes! Fortunately, in this case, we were able to negotiate a deal with the IRS that enabled the transaction to go through.

A lien can also be attached to your business property, including accounts receivable! I know of a situation where a small business owner walked into a restaurant to get some lunch, and when he returned to the parking lot, he found his work truck was being towed away to the impound lot. It turned out the IRS was so frustrated with him that they confiscated his vehicle with the intention to sell it and use the proceeds to pay his tax bill. These situations can and do happen!

The federal tax lien is so powerful that it may affect your ability to get credit, and it may continue even after you file bankruptcy! There are, however, a few ways the IRS will allow you to deal with a lien. They are:

1. **Paying off your tax debt.** This must be the full amount, of course.

2. **A discharge.** This is the most ideal, as it removes the lien entirely from specific property. However, there are a limited number of situations where it is possible.

3. **A subordination.** This doesn't remove the lien; it just allows other creditors to have a higher priority than the IRS. It can be useful when

getting a mortgage. Again, certain conditions must be met for this to be an option.

4. **A withdrawal.** This one is great because it completely removes the lien from public records. Naturally, there is fine print (catching on to a trend here?).

All this to say, liens are not good and it's best to avoid them. Fortunately, you do have some options if you're in a position where a Notice of Federal Tax Lien has been filed.

Now, let's dig a bit deeper into the concept of a levy. Basically, a levy is when the IRS takes your stuff. However, they can only take property that exists on the date of the levy, so it's usually a one-time deal. An exception is a levy on your salary, which is also called a wage garnishment. This type of penalty is continuous and generally is only removed once the IRS has collected the total amount it's owed.

The good news is that the IRS *must* give you a Notice of Intent to Levy before the levy is made. The challenge? People don't open their mail, so they don't even know a levy is about to happen! I'll talk about the importance of opening your mail later in this chapter.

There are some things that are exempt from the levy. Unemployment benefits, workers' compensation payments, and court-ordered child support are some examples. Even with these exemptions, make no mistake, the IRS has a lot of power in this area and can place a levy on a wide variety of items.

The most common levy I see is a bank levy. This happens when the IRS contacts your bank and takes all the money in your account to pay your outstanding tax bill. This situation is really the pits. Visualize going to your bank to withdraw money only to find out there is nothing there. Yikes! Unfortunately, it happens all the time.

Another type of levy is a seizure. This is when the IRS takes your property (a car, for example), sells it, and uses the proceeds to pay down your tax debt. Have you ever walked out of the grocery store and not remembered where you parked? Imagine what it would feel like if you could never find your car because the IRS towed it away, leaving you standing in the parking lot holding your grocery bags. Not a comfy feeling.

If you want to avoid the possibility of a levy, the best thing to do is work with the IRS as soon as you know there's a problem. However, if you do receive a formal levy notice, you can often prevent the levy if the notice is brought to your tax resolution specialist early enough. Levy prevention requires specific forms to be filed in a certain order. One misstep can be detrimental to your entire situation. The most important thing to remember is that you need to open your mail!

OPEN YOUR MAIL!

A gentleman named Ted called me and said, "The IRS just took all my savings! I logged into my online bank account and found my $10,000 balance was now at zero! How can they do that without even telling me?"

"Well," I began, "The IRS *is* required to notify you before they levy your bank account or garnish your wages. Are you sure you didn't receive a certified letter from the IRS recently?"

"I'm too scared to open any letters from the IRS," Ted said. "I just throw them in the trash. Don't they have to call me or email me or something?"

Oh boy, I thought. *This guy has been avoiding the IRS and hoping something like this wouldn't happen. He's not going to like my answer.*

"Ted, all those letters you threw away? That *was* the IRS telling you they were going to take money from you! If you'd opened your mail, I could have prevented this from happening, given the proper notice. Now the money is long gone, and it's doubtful that we'll get it back!" I said.

I've mentioned this several times so far, and it bears repeating. It is of the utmost importance that you open letters mailed to you from the IRS. These letters often have a deadline on them that, if missed, will take your case from bad to worse. Not only that, but some of these letters have a ticking clock and if we are able to react within a certain amount of time, we can contact a department in the IRS that may expedite the entire process. There is a real potential for a positive outcome if this happens!

In another situation, a lady named Missy came to me very upset because of a bank levy. Missy said she was 100 percent certain the IRS had never mailed her anything before they took money out of her bank account. I explained that the IRS will not do that. She vehemently disagreed with me, reeling from the fact that the funds the IRS took were intended to pay for her monthly mortgage.

After some discussion, I discovered that Missy had moved a few years ago, and since she hadn't filed any tax returns with her new address, the letters the IRS was trying to send her were being mailed to the wrong house. The IRS had, in fact, been complying with the notification law and sending letters to Missy's last known address, but the problem was that they'd never been informed of her new address.

OOPS! Tip: The IRS will use your most recent tax return, a written statement, an oral notification, or a change of address form as your last known address. If you move, I highly recommend you complete and send in a Form 8822 Change of Address form. Remember that a simple address forwarding will expire and is not enough to update the IRS on your change of address.

In Missy's case, we made the argument that she needed the money the IRS levied to pay her mortgage. Luckily, the appeal was successful because we were able to provide the appropriate financial documentation proving an immediate economic hardship. This isn't always easy to pull off, but it can be effective in the right situations. Eventually, we set Missy up on an installment agreement with payments that she could afford.

By now, you should understand that if you fail to fulfill your tax obligations, you are putting yourself and your family in harm's way. Mistakes happen; I get it. We're all human beings with a lot going on, but when you ignore the IRS's warning shots after you have an oops moment, it will only cost you more time, money, and anguish.

Please take immediate action; tax problems don't just go away on their own.

CHAPTER 5

The OOPS! Process Revealed

According to a recent survey, 12 percent of Americans
say it's fine to cheat a little on your taxes,
while the other 88 percent know not to talk to a guy
with a clipboard asking them if they cheat on their taxes.
— **JIMMY FALLON**

Now you must decide. Are you willing to invest the time and effort necessary to fix your tax problem once and for all? Do you want peace of mind knowing that you and your family are safe and protected? Would you like to walk to your mailbox knowing no matter what's in there, you'll be okay? You haven't been getting much sleep lately, have you? Let's change that. Do not take this decision lightly. If you're ready to experience the freedom of having this IRS burden off your shoulders, read on.

Understanding the OOPS! process detailed in Chapter Two is a great place to start when addressing your tax issues. However, it's crucial that you complete the steps in sequential order. In this chapter, I'll walk you through each step and exactly what needs to be done before you move on to the next one. Recall the four steps:

1. Organize your records.
2. Observe the tax laws and get compliant.
3. Patch up the damage that was done.
4. Safeguard against future problems.

STEP 1: ORGANIZE YOUR RECORDS

The first step in the OOPS! process is to organize your records. Before you can take any other action, it's critical to know what your financial picture looks like as well as where you stand with the IRS. I know these two topics are scary, uncomfortable, and boring for most, but you must know your starting point before moving toward resolution.

First, if you have letters from the IRS, gather them together and locate the most recent one. All the letters are important, but the most recent one will tell you how much the IRS claims you owe them and for which years. Examine this letter carefully. Is there a deadline to respond? Write this date on your calendar for later. Does the year and the fact that the IRS believes you owe them something for that year make sense? Note this as well. The answer to this question will help determine our path forward.

Next, assemble your personal financial information. Get bank statements for each of your accounts, paystubs from your job, and any documents related to your assets such as house mortgage, cars, retirement accounts, etc. Use these documents to determine your net income (what you make minus what you spend) and your net worth (what you own minus what you owe). Write these figures down. We will use them in a future step. If this part is confusing, don't worry. I'll give you step-by-step instructions to calculate your net income and net worth in Chapter Six.

If you have a small business, pull your business net income and net worth from your bookkeeping software. Don't have it? No problem. You'll use your business bank statements and go through the same net income and net worth exercise in Chapter Six to get these figures.

OOPS! Tip: If you have a business but not a separate business checking account, *you need to open one today!* Mixing personal and business expenses in one account is a sin against your legitimacy as a business owner. Separating your personal and business transactions into two different accounts will give you a clearer picture of how your business is doing.

Congratulations! The first step in the OOPS! process is complete! That wasn't so hard now, was it? At this point, you should know how much the IRS claims you owe them, for what tax years, whether you agree that you owe something for those years, the next deadline for your response, and what your net income and net worth are.

STEP 2: OBSERVE THE TAX LAWS AND GET COMPLIANT

The second step in the OOPS! process is to observe the tax laws and get compliant. Compliance boils down to filing all required forms (for most, this will be your annual tax return) and getting up-to-date on paying the IRS for taxes on your current income.

Let's say you've been a little lax on filing your annual 1040 tax return and haven't filed in the last three years. Another possibility is that you're a business with employees and payroll, and you haven't filed your payroll tax returns like you're supposed to. In both scenarios, you're out of compliance with your filings.

Why is this important? I'm going to let you in on a little secret: the IRS is not going to let you set up any sort of payment plan or permanent resolution option until you are in compliance with your tax filings! This tip alone will save you at least one phone call with the IRS. You'll be ahead of the game compared to other people who call the IRS to set up a payment plan only to be denied for their lack of compliance. You're welcome.

The next phase of this step is to get up-to-date on paying the IRS the taxes you owe on your current income. I'm not talking about the past-due balance you determined in Step 1: Organize. I'm referring to establishing proper withholdings from your paycheck or paying estimated quarterly tax payments if you have a business. This shows the IRS that you've "stopped the bleeding" and won't incur another tax liability this year.

OOPS! Tip: Taxes are not due at the end of the year when you file your return. You read that right. Taxes must be paid as you earn or receive income throughout the year, either through withholding or estimated tax payments. If you don't do this, you can be subject to penalties and interest!

Ignoring this phase could hinder your ability to obtain a final resolution from the IRS as well. The IRS wants to see that you have "righted the ship" for the current year and won't owe them even more than you already do.

If you're an employee and don't think you're having enough taxes withheld from your paycheck, ask your payroll department for a Form W-4 and have them take even more of your paycheck for taxes. If you have a small business or are getting paid as a 1099 individual contractor, it's critical that you make quarterly estimated tax payments. This can be done by mailing the IRS a check with a voucher or paying your estimated tax balance online.

OOPS! Tip: The IRS.gov website has a Tax Withholding Estimator. Use this tool anytime during the year to see if you're having enough taxes withheld from your paycheck or are paying enough in estimated tax payments. This is a great tool, and I'd recommend everyone do this!

Okay, now you are cooking with oil! The second step is complete, and you are ready to move on with your resolution and quest for freedom!

STEP 3: PATCH UP THE DAMAGE THAT WAS DONE

The third step in the OOPS! process is to patch up the damage that was done. This is where the rubber meets the road. The first two steps — Organize and Observe — have prepared you for the third step, which involves contacting the IRS. You knew this had to be done at some point, and now is the time. Don't worry; I'll walk you through what to say to them to get a favorable resolution.

In this section, I'll discuss three primary resolution techniques and how they may apply to your situation. Ranging in difficulty from the most complicated to the easiest, the techniques are: offer in compromise (OIC), currently not collectible (CNC), and an installment agreement. I'll give you an overview here and do a deeper dive in Chapter 9.

Offer in Compromise

The IRS OIC program is arguably the most lucrative option in our toolbox because it allows you to settle your tax debt for less than the full amount you owe. This also makes it the most difficult to qualify for. Statistically, only about 40 percent of all offers submitted to the IRS are accepted. Yikes! Remember: the IRS is not in the business of giving away money — quite the opposite.

Before pursuing an OIC, you must first determine if you are even eligible to apply. The initial requirements are:

1. All your required tax returns must be filed, and estimated tax payments must be current. This should be complete since you've finished the second step in the OOPS! process (Observe).
2. You can't be in an open bankruptcy proceeding.
3. If you have employees, you must have made payroll tax deposits for the current and last two quarters.

If you meet all the requirements above, you are eligible to apply for an OIC! However, the process of submission, review, and approval can take more than nine months to complete. You'll need persistence and lots of patience, so hang in there.

Currently Not Collectible

The next resolution technique is the currently not collectible status or CNC. If you do not qualify for an OIC, or if your offer was rejected or returned and there's just no way you can pay your IRS debt, a CNC may be the way to go.

With a CNC, the IRS puts a temporary hold on your account until your current financial condition improves. This status doesn't mean your debt goes away permanently; it simply provides you with some immediate relief from making any payments.

An important consideration with a CNC is that you'll need to prove to the IRS that you truly cannot afford to make monthly payments in any amount. If you have money left in your bank account at the end of the month, the IRS is going to want it. You should only consider a CNC if there is just no way to pay anything right now. Even if you can get into a CNC status, the IRS will eventually review your ability to pay and take you out of CNC if your financial picture has improved.

Installment Agreement

The last option for patching up the damage to your tax standing is an installment agreement. Also called a payment plan, this is what you'll need to establish with the IRS to pay off your tax debt if you didn't qualify for an OIC or CNC.

Similar to the OIC and CNC strategies, you must be current on your tax filings and have the appropriate amount of taxes withheld from your paycheck or be making estimated tax payments in order to qualify. This is because the IRS wants to ensure that you won't incur a tax liability for the current and preferably future years.

The primary benefit of setting up an installment agreement is that the IRS won't garnish your wages or levy your bank account while you have an active agreement and are making the payments. With an installment agreement, you'll know exactly what the monthly payment amount is, and you are controlling the cash flow, not the IRS. There's also a clear end date (your last payment) when your tax balance will be zero. However, like the CNC, penalties and interest will accrue, and the IRS will take any future tax refunds and apply them to your balance.

As you can see, there are positives and negatives to an installment agreement, but all in all, it's a viable resolution option that will get you out of the crosshairs of the IRS.

At this point, you should have a resolution option in place, and the IRS shouldn't be hounding you anymore. Yay! You did it! Look back at how far you've come — from being afraid to go to your mailbox to having a resolution in place for your tax problem and a clear path to freedom. Now, let's keep it that way.

STEP 4: SAFEGUARD AGAINST FUTURE TAX PROBLEMS

The final step in the OOPS! process is to safeguard against future tax problems. This step is not about stashing cash in the Cayman Islands or opening a Swiss bank account. It's about the basics of bookkeeping and transaction management so you don't get in trouble with the IRS again. Before you can graduate to implementing the tax strategies of the super-rich, you must first master the basics!

If you are a full-time employee, this means having the right amount of taxes withheld from your paycheck. Many believe that if you work for someone else, the company is responsible for withholding the right amount of federal and state income tax from your paycheck. This is technically not true! While your employer *is* responsible for paying the federal and state agencies the amount withheld, it is your responsibility to tell them how much to withhold.

If you are self-employed, you have an added challenge. No one else is going to withhold taxes from your pay throughout the year. You must do this on your own. How? By submitting quarterly estimated tax payments. I talked about quarterly tax payments earlier in this chapter, but if you need a refresher, go back to Step 2: Observe the Tax Laws and Get Compliant.

For businesses with employees or subcontractors, tax compliance is a whole different ball of wax. I highly recommend finding a qualified professional to take care of your tax reporting and payment obligations. I know it costs money. I know it's a pain in the butt. But this pain pales in comparison to the pain you'll feel if the IRS reaches out to you!

Another way to stay compliant with your tax obligation is to — wait for it — file your annual tax return and pay any balance due on time! This is the best indicator available to determine whether you're getting into hot water. It's a lagging indicator but a good one, nonetheless. Ignoring your annual tax returns is a surefire way to get the attention of the IRS. Don't do it.

Safeguarding against future problems doesn't just involve getting compliant with your taxes. You'll also need to implement a bookkeeping strategy. If you are self-employed, you need to keep track of what you make and what you spend. The best way to start is with a dedicated business bank account. Then, track everything, and don't use your business account for personal transactions. It's okay to use a simple Excel spreadsheet to track your finances when you're first starting out. All you have to do is transfer income and expenses from your bank statement to the spreadsheet so you can see how your business is performing and what you need to report on your tax return at the end of the year.

Finally, I'll say this once again: make sure the IRS knows your current address, and open your mail! I understand it can be nerve-wracking but do it anyway. Don't ever put yourself in a position where the IRS thinks you're hiding from them.

There you have it. The OOPS! process in its full glory! In the next chapters, I'll give you additional details about how to implement each step of the process and provide some helpful nuggets to guide you on your journey to freedom.

CHAPTER 6

Do This First

What kind of taxes are on trash bags?
Hefty ones, and no one is Glad about it.

A lady called me once and said she'd recently received a letter from the IRS stating that she owed more than $300,000. I told her to get me the letter so I could review it. Upon further investigation, it turned out that the IRS didn't allow any of her business expenses to offset her income because the records (or lack thereof) that were given to the IRS were a mess. Since the IRS couldn't make heads or tails of her records, all expenses were denied, and she'd been assessed.

Keeping clean, organized records can go a long way with the IRS. I can't stress this point enough. Chances are the situation you're in is due, at least in part, to being unorganized. Fortunately, you can start the process of getting organized now, even if you've already received letters from the IRS. Let's take a deeper dive into the first step in the OOPS! process: Getting organized.

LETTER-OPENING PARTY

If I've said this once, I've said it a thousand times: open your mail! We're no longer ducking, hiding, bobbing, and weaving. Take a deep breath and rip the Band-Aid off. It's time for you to have a letter-opening party of one! Grab some snacks, a beverage, and a letter opener, and rip those suckers open. Don't worry about the contents just yet; simply focus on getting through them all. Unfold the papers in each envelope, use a paper clip to group them together, sort them by date, and stack them face up with newer letters on the bottom.

Starting with the letter on top (the oldest one), read through it in its entirety. Take note of the date, tax year, and amount the IRS claims you owe. Now set this letter aside, face up, and read the next one. Reviewing the second letter will go a little faster since there's some repetitive language, especially toward the end. When you're finished reading, place this second letter face up on top of the first one.

Repeat this process until you've read all the IRS letters. Why did we do this? To help you understand the sequence of actions the IRS has taken up to this point and so you can know what tax year(s) and amount(s) the IRS is asking for.

Look at the most current letter on top of the pile. Observe the notice number in the upper right corner of the page. There are dozens of notice numbers the IRS uses, ranging from a CP14 (*hey, you owe us some money*) to a CP504, followed by an LT11 notice or a Letter 1058 (*we are about to drain your bank account!*). It's best to act quickly no matter what notice you get, but if you receive one of these last two letters, you're sitting on a ticking time bomb. If you don't do something before the due date on these letters, the IRS will take your stuff.

OOPS! Tip: Notice numbers are important because they indicate how far along the collection process you are with the IRS. These numbers will dictate the best next steps for resolution.

While this book is about how to solve your tax problem on your own, if you get a CP504, LT11, or Letter 1058, I highly recommend seeking help from a qualified professional. You are now dead in the IRS's crosshairs, and they are done firing warning shots — the next one will be a direct hit.

The last step of your letter-opening party is to write down a summary of the most current

IRS letter. Note the years they're looking for, the amounts for each year, and the type of tax the liability relates to (most will be income tax). Add all the years together to get the total amount owed and set this number aside.

YOUR INCOME STATEMENT

Next, let's get a handle on your financial picture. We'll start by putting together your income statement (how much money you make minus how much you spend). Gather your bank statements from the last three months, credit card statements, and employment paystubs. Grab some lined paper or create an Excel spreadsheet and write "Monthly gross income" on the first line. If you don't want to create the spreadsheet from scratch, go to BPBTaxResolutions.com/Book, where you can get a free template that I've put together for you. Use your paystub to calculate a three-month average of your gross pay (the amount you made before taxes and deductions) and enter this figure to the right of the words you just wrote. If you're married and file joint taxes with your spouse, you should include their income as part of this calculation.

On the next line down, write "Expenses." We'll create several line items in the expense section, and you'll get most of these amounts from your bank and credit card statements, again using three-month averages.

The first expense line will be "Mortgage/Rent." Write this below the Expense heading. Calculate the average of the last three months' expenses for your home mortgage or rent and write this figure to the right of the Mortgage/Rent line (this number should appear under the income figure you've already written down).

On the next line down, write "Utilities." Again, take the three-month average of all your home utilities such as electricity, gas, water, trash, cell phone, TV, lawn care, etc. Add this number to the right of the Utilities label. Hopefully, you are getting the hang of this now!

In a row beneath Utilities, continue with the following line items: Food and clothing (include cleaning supplies), Car payments (one per car), Car expenses (include insurance, fuel, maintenance), Health insurance (medical and dental), Medical expenses, Life insurance, Student loan payments, Taxes (federal, state, social security, and Medicare), and Other (everything not in any line items above).

Write the three-month average cost of each line item listed, just like you did for Mortgage/Rent and Utilities. On the next row, write "Total Expenses" and add all the expense numbers together. On the row under Total Expenses, write Net Income. To get this number, subtract the total expenses from your income on the very first row.

The spreadsheet you created should look something like this:

Monthly gross income	$8,000
Expenses:	
Mortgage	$1,800
Utilities	$600
Car payment #1	$500
Car payment #2	$400
Car expenses	$500
Health insurance	$600
Medical costs	$100
Life insurance	$100
Student loan	$200
Taxes	$2,500
Other	$400
Total expenses	$7,700
Net income	$300

That's it! You now know exactly how much money you have left at the end of each month. Generally, the IRS will use this number plus the amount in your

"Other" expense line (the IRS calls these expenses non-allowable) to help determine what type of payment plan you can afford.

YOUR NET WORTH

Next, let's determine your net worth. On another sheet of paper or in Excel, write the word "Assets" at the top left. Under this line, we'll list all the things you own that have financial value. If you own your house (even if it has a mortgage), write that first with the value of the house to the right. To obtain the value, use the sales price of the house if you purchased it recently; if not, use an online valuing service such as Zillow.

Create another column to the right of Assets and label it "Liabilities." Under this heading, we'll list any loans you have. To figure the liability of your house, write the current balance of your mortgage. You can get this from your most recent monthly mortgage statement sent to you by your bank. If you have a home equity line of credit with a balance, make a new line for this as well.

Next, let's fill in some other common assets and liabilities. If you purchased your car, write "Car" under the "House" line item. To value your car, look it up with an online service like Kelly Blue Book. Write the result under the Assets column and then find the current balance (if any) that you owe to the bank for the car. Write "Car Loan" and this number under the Liabilities column. If you have more than one car, add a line for each additional car under the first car. In the event you have a car with no loan, enter the car value under Assets and leave the Liabilities blank. If you are leasing a car, do not enter anything for it.

List any bank accounts and their respective balances under assets. This would be checking accounts, savings accounts, CDs, and the like. Below all your bank accounts, list any investment accounts such as IRAs, 401ks, stock brokerage accounts, etc. If there are any loans against these accounts, enter those amounts under Liabilities.

Finally, list any other assets, such as rental homes, boats, or valuable collections, along with any associated loans against those assets. Don't worry about furniture or electronics unless they are highly valuable. Now, list any other liabilities you have, like secured loans, personal loans, or credit cards.

Now add up the Assets and Liabilities figures and subtract the Liabilities from Assets to get your Net Worth. Generally, the IRS isn't going to allow you to use credit card debt to reduce your assets, so they will add that amount back into the total to get a final Net Worth figure. This is the amount the IRS thinks you have available to give them to satisfy your tax debt. Your Net Worth statement should look something like this:

Assets		Liabilities	
House	$250,000	Mortgage	$150,000
Car	$20,000	HELOC	$50,000
Spouse car	$30,000	Car loan	$15,000
Checking acct	$1,000	Spouse car loan	$25,000
Savings acct	$5,000	401k loan	$5,000
IRA	$10,000	Credit cards	$11,000
Spouse 401k	$25,000	Rental home mtg	$120,000
Rental home	$150,000		
Total Assets	**$491,000**	**Total Liabilities**	**$376,000**

Net Worth	$115,000

Whew! I know that exercise took a lot of time and effort, but look at what you've accomplished! You have a good handle on where your money is coming from, where it's going, what's left over, how much you've saved, and how much you owe others. Not only is this important to have when you call the IRS, but it's also important to have for your own financial well-being!

I recommend that everyone go through this process on a monthly basis so you always know where you stand financially. This way, you can identify and quickly plug any holes in your financial boat. If you don't enjoy using spreadsheets or calculating these totals by hand, there are lots of free software programs out there to help you capture, track, and report your personal financial information. Check out my list of recommended tools at BPBTaxResolutions.com/Book.

SMALL BUSINESS BOOKKEEPING

If you have a small business, you'll need to prepare the books for your business before you can start calculating your income statements and net worth. This is where having a separate bank account for your business will pay off big time. It is so much easier to create an income statement and net worth for your company when your business transactions are not comingled with your personal expenses.

First, you'll need to go through your business transactions, line by line, and categorize them by an expense type that's unique to your business. Add all the transactions for each expense type together and put them on your income statement. The income statement will look like your personal one, just with different expense line items.

Next, create a net worth statement (commonly known as a balance sheet) for your business. Again, this will look similar to your personal net worth, but the line items and totals will list business assets and liabilities. Once complete, you'll have a financial picture for your small business!

To avoid any accidental over- or under-reporting, make sure you don't double count any income or expense item on your personal and business financial statements. Each financial transaction should be either personal or business, but not both. Like my recommendation for your personal financial statements, I'd recommend preparing your business financial statements on a monthly basis.

OOPS! Tip: Most of you are not bookkeepers, and preparing the books for your business would be considered a low-value activity. You'd be better served by spending your time marketing and selling your product or service. Hire someone else to take care of your books!

You should now have a good handle on your small business and personal financial picture. Just look at the progress you've made! I'm proud of your resolve to get to this point. I know it wasn't easy. Now that you know your numbers, take a look at the most recent IRS letter you've set aside. There is likely to be a deadline listed on the first page. Put this deadline in your calendar so you don't miss it. We'll go through what to do in the next chapter.

CHAPTER 7

It May Not Be Your Fault, but It Is Your Problem

*The income tax created more criminals than
any other single act of government.*
— **BARRY GOLDWATER**.

Even if you follow my advice to open every letter the IRS sends you, the contents of that letter may still come as a shock. This is what happened to my client Rita, who called me and said, "The IRS is claiming I owe them $24,000 from three years ago. I have no idea what this is for. We *always* filed and paid our taxes on time!"

Rita was a very friendly, loving mother of two kids, a boy and a girl. She'd stayed home to raise her children while finishing her teaching degree at a local university. Her husband, Dale, worked as a project manager in a large corporation and was the sole breadwinner during this time.

Unfortunately, Rita and Dale's relationship became quite strained due to the challenges of raising a family and the demands of Dale's job. They divorced about a year ago and Rita, teaching degree in hand, got a job at the kids' elementary school.

After talking with Rita, we determined that the tax year with the outstanding $24,000 balance was from when Rita and Dale were still married and had filed a joint return. I had my suspicions about this one but needed more information. Rita hired me, and I did some digging.

As it turned out, Rita and Dale had filed on time, but the tax due wasn't paid. In addition, three years of penalties and interest were stacking up daily, making the balance grow even more.

"Dale said he paid that on time!" Rita said when I broke the news to her. "This was his responsibility, not mine. I shouldn't be on the hook for this!" she added.

Rita and I looked at a copy of the original tax return. "Is this your signature on the return?" I asked.

"Yes," she responded.

"And this is Dale's, right?" I continued.

"Yes, it is," Rita replied.

"Then it's both of your problems," I told her.

"That's not fair! Dale was the one in charge of taking care of our finances. My job was to be home with the kids!" Rita exclaimed.

"I understand," I said in my most empathetic tone. "But in the eyes of the IRS, that doesn't matter. They're going to come after both of you for this debt."

In the end, I was able to set up a reasonable payment plan with the IRS for Rita. However, the IRS will still be going after Dale as long as there is an outstanding balance.

OOPS! Tip: When two taxpayers are married and file a joint return, they have what's called a *joint and several liability.* This means that each taxpayer is legally responsible for the entire debt, even if you've divorced after you filed a joint tax return.

I've lost track of how many times I've heard this sad story from people across all walks of life. Their situations include everything from "My husband bought a boat with the money we set aside for taxes" to "Why is the IRS taxing the debt I defaulted on?" So, please let this be a lesson to you. No matter how much you love your spouse, how great your relationship is, or how busy you are with life, you can trust but verify. It is a loving and respectful act to be open with your spouse regarding finances. You should both be involved when reviewing and filing your tax returns.

In my experience, one person is usually responsible for managing the household finances and making sure taxes are filed and paid. If this is you, please get your spouse involved, even if it's just at a high level. If this is not your role, get involved. Do yourself a favor and have this talk with your spouse today. You will thank me later for it.

Now, look carefully at those IRS letters you've been gathering. Is your name and social security number listed? If so, regardless of what transpired to get to this point, you have a problem and it's on you to get it resolved.

OOPS! Tip: The IRS considers a loan you've defaulted on as taxable income. For example, if you stop paying your car loan and the bank writes it off, they will send you a Form 1099-C Cancellation of Debt for the amount written off that must be reported on your tax return as income. So, if you think walking away from your car loan will not cost you anything, think again!

Even if you're on the same page as your spouse when it comes to your finances, debt, and taxes, there are so many reasons people decide to forgo paying the IRS what's owed.

I've heard, "I just can't afford to pay my taxes," from people who drive a new BMW.

"Can't you just explain to the IRS that I had a bad year?" (This was the tenth year in a row, FYI.)

"My dog died."

"I got a flat tire."

"I don't like the IRS."

"Taylor Swift was in town."

Okay, I made that last one up, but you catch my drift. The IRS doesn't give a hoot about these little things. For the bigger events in life, however, like the death of a close family member or a serious illness, there are some ways to get a little leeway from the IRS. For the most part, though, if you make money, you owe taxes. Period.

FALSE ASSUMPTIONS AND BELIEFS ABOUT PAYING TAXES

While every story has its own unique twist, almost all these people have one thing in common: their false assumptions and beliefs about getting straight with the IRS. They just don't think it is possible and want to give up hope. Read on to discover the truth behind some of the false assumptions and beliefs I encounter in my profession.

The Internal Revenue Service Hasn't Contacted Me, So I Should Be Okay.

This is probably the most dangerous false assumption. Just because you haven't heard from the IRS doesn't mean you don't have a balance with them. Yes, the IRS is supposed to let you know if you owe them money; however, this communication doesn't always reach you. The IRS could be sending you letters that are going to an old address and not being forwarded to you (remember Missy from Chapter 4?). Or perhaps you're ignoring these letters and waiting for the IRS to call or email you because "that's when you know it's a real problem." Think again. Letters from the IRS signify there *is* a problem!

OOPS! Tip: The IRS does not initiate contact with taxpayers by email, text messages, or social media to request personal or financial information. Be aware of scammers!

A few years ago, a gentleman named Richard called and told me he hadn't filed his tax returns in more than five years. He was surprised that he'd flown under the radar for such a long time and knew it wouldn't last. I agreed, and asked why he was reaching out to me now.

"I just can't sleep," he said. "I feel like there's a piano dangling over me that's hanging on by a thread, and I can't handle it anymore. Plus, I'm going to get married soon, and my fiancé told me she won't marry me until I get right with the IRS."

"I commend you for this," I told him. "Not only are you having an up-front conversation with your fiancé about finances before getting married, but you're also taking action to do something about it." I really appreciate people like this who recognize they've made a mistake and own up to it.

Richard continued explaining his situation to me. "I've discarded all the tax documentation that was sent to me these past few years, so I don't even have anything to give you."

"It's okay," I told him. "We can retrieve your wage and income transcripts from the years you need to file. I just need your authorization to get them from the IRS."

"Okay, where do I sign?" he said.

We were able to get his back tax returns filed, abate some penalties, and set this guy up on a monthly payment plan with the IRS that he could afford. They're getting married next year.

OOPS! Tip: Penalty abatement refers to removing penalties that were imposed by the IRS. Certain conditions must be met to qualify for penalty abatement, but it can be an effective way to save money.

I'm Just a Little Fish, Why Doesn't the Internal Revenue Service Just Focus on Those Big Corporations?

Oh yes, this is a good one. Do you want to know why the IRS doesn't only zero in on those big corporations? Because of the federal tax gap!

OOPS! Tip: The federal tax gap is the difference between what taxpayers owe in a year and what is actually paid on time. This is a huge income opportunity for the IRS!

The IRS estimates that the tax gap in 2023 is $625 billion! Not only that, but they believe 74 percent of the tax gap is made up of individual filers.[3]

To give you some perspective on how much $625 billion is, the entire federal government budget is about $6 trillion. This means that every 10 years the government could be fully funded with just the amount of money the IRS is owed but hasn't collected! Every little bit counts and adds up to a big amount, so you bet the IRS is going after the "little fish" — there are a lot of them!

---

3 "IRS Estimates a $625 Billion Tax Gap." Committee for a Responsible Federal Budget, October 24, 2023. https://www.crfb.org/blogs/irs-estimates-625-billion-tax-gap

I Heard About a Guy Who Made a Deal with the IRS and Got His Balance Removed Entirely! Let's Just Make the IRS an Offer They Can't Refuse!

Remember the game "telephone" you played when you were in elementary school? The class sat in a circle, and the teacher whispered a sentence in one student's ear. Then, that kid whispered the same message in the ear of the student to their right. This continued around the entire circle, and when the last kid heard the message, they would say out loud what they'd heard.

How many times was the last message the exact same as the first message? *Never.* The story changed practically every time it was whispered! Do you see why I'm telling you this? The sweet deal you heard someone else got from the IRS is likely very different from reality.

In addition, every situation is unique. Your circumstances are going to be different, and there are many nuances to each case that can drastically alter the outcome. Just because someone was able to get a reduction in their balance doesn't necessarily mean that you can.

Yes, the IRS grants offers that reduce the liability of some taxpayers. However, just one number out of place or one comment said the wrong way could be the difference between acceptance and rejection. Offers are very delicate, and if you don't know what you are doing, irreparable damage could be done.

Take the success stories that you hear with a grain of salt. Realize that everyone has a different scenario and an OIC is not the best resolution in all situations.

Getting Help Is Just Too Expensive.

There may be a point in your journey where you are too overwhelmed to move forward. You want to give up because you think you have no other options. I understand why you feel this way. The IRS is a powerful entity, and they don't mess around. Tax law, numbers, finances, income statements, net worth — it can all be very confusing.

Your financial future may be hanging in the balance, and the decisions you make could impact the next few years or the remainder of your life. Remember that not doing anything is the worst move. Hesitating not only costs you money but also takes an emotional toll on you. There is no way of quantifying lost sleep, anxiety, and strained relationships.

Please recognize that hiring a qualified professional might be your best option. Working with someone who knows the IRS playbook, the proper order of events that must take place for a successful resolution, and the right words to use and when to use them could save you money in the long run.

Take Ron, for example, a middle-aged gentleman who received a letter from the IRS and came to see me for help. After talking to him about his options and our pricing, he balked and said he'd just take care of the problem himself. His scenario was complex, and I was confident we could get a good resolution for him, but he stood firm in his decision.

About a year later, he called me up. "This is just too daunting. I want to push the *easy button*. Will you still help me?" he asked.

"I'd be happy to, Ron. Bring in any letters you've recently received from the IRS, and let's put a game plan together," I responded.

As I originally suspected, this was a complex case. Nonetheless, we were able to get a favorable resolution with the IRS and save Ron a good chunk of money. I didn't have the heart to tell Ron, but the penalties and interest he accrued during the year he waited to move forward with me was greater than my fee.

Don't hesitate to get your tax problem addressed. Each day costs you money. Act now.

CHAPTER 8

Making It Rain

Worried about an IRS audit? Avoid what's called a red flag.
That's something the IRS always looks for.
For example, say you have some money left in your
bank account after paying taxes; that's a red flag.
— JAY LENO

For those of you who own a small business, there's an important idea that I'd like you to wrap your head around. Even if you don't, this is a good bit of information to have in your back pocket. It's an economic concept called *opportunity cost*. Many people only associate opportunity cost with business decisions, but it is just as important in your personal life.

OOPS! Tip: An *opportunity cost* is the loss of potential gain from other alternatives when one alternative is chosen. For example, if you spend your time and money going to the casino, then you are choosing not to spend your time reading a book or your money on investing in your retirement account.

Back in my younger years, I wanted to save money by changing the oil in my car on my own. I bought a book explaining what tools I needed and what steps to take. After fumbling about a bit the first few times, I finally got the process down and was able to perform the entire routine without too much trouble.

Even though I was able to finish the oil change without breaking anything major, it still took some time to complete. I had to drive to the auto parts store to purchase new oil, an oil filter, and a new drain plug washer, then drive home.

Then I had to place the car ramps under my rear wheels and back the car up to the top of the ramps, but not too far, or the car would fall off (something that almost happened once!). Next, I'd have to crawl under the car ,place the oil pan beneath the drain plug, and unscrew the plug until the old oil drained out.

After that, I'd use an oil filter wrench to remove the old oil filter and replace it with the new one. Then I'd screw the oil drain plug back in, along with a new drain plug washer. The car was a bit older, so the oil drain plug and oil filter were relatively easy to access.

Once everything was back in place, I could carefully drive the car forward off the ramps and park it. Then I'd opened the hood, remove the oil cap, and fill the engine with the recommended amount of new oil before replacing the oil cap and checking the dipstick to make sure I'd added the proper amount of oil.

Finally, it was time to check for leaks. This meant starting the car, letting it run for just a bit, and checking under the car for puddles. If there were no leaks, the oil change was complete, and I just had to properly dispose of the used oil. If there was a leak, I had to drive the car back up on the ramps and diagnose the problem. Usually, any issues were the result of a loose oil drain plug, which required a torque wrench to tighten properly — something I'd never bought because I figured a regular socket set worked fine.

From start (driving to the auto parts store) to finish (putting all the tools away and washing up), I'd spend roughly two hours changing my oil — if I didn't encounter any difficulties.

Please note that this is not a complete guide on how to change the oil in your car, as I've left out many details for the sake of conversation. Why did I tell you this story, then? I'm getting to that!

During the time in my life when I was changing the oil in my own car, I was working at a job that paid me an hourly wage. Most days, I had the chance to work overtime and get paid about $16 per hour (it was the early 1990s, mind you), which also impressed my boss. The cost of a professional oil change was $19.99.

By choosing to "save money" and change the oil in my car, I was forgoing the opportunity to make $32 ($16 an hour for 2 hours). Back out the $19.99, I could pay someone else, and I'm still up twelve bucks. That's opportunity cost. This scenario doesn't even account for the clothes I stained with oil, the cuts and bruises I got on my hands, and the spills that I made on my garage floor.

I realize this is a small, simple example, but it can be applied to so many areas of your personal life, such as mowing your lawn, cleaning your house, and picking up your dog's poop. Basically, if you can pay someone else to complete simple, time-consuming tasks while you spend your precious time on higher-value work or even on something that gives you great enjoyment, do it!

Some people find joy in mowing their grass, cleaning their house, or changing the oil in their car. If this is you, then by all means, keep doing it! I just ask that you calculate the opportunity cost to see if it's worth it to you from a financial standpoint.

Let's apply the concept of opportunity cost to your small business. I've spoken to dozens of business owners who are hell-bent on saving money by preparing their own tax returns or doing their own books. In the beginning, I get it. You're bootstrapping just to get off the ground and save money so you can reinvest in the business. However, you need to hire out these administrative tasks as soon as you possibly can because instead of saving money, you're actually missing out on the opportunity to make even more.

You are the rainmaker. Your job is to put money in the bank, not put numbers in boxes. The most critical part of growing your business is to spend time on marketing and sales. Advertising your business, meeting with prospects, and closing deals are where your time is needed most! If you could spend a few hundred dollars a month to get your books done and use that time to make a few *thousand* dollars a month making it rain, that's a no-brainer, isn't it? Of course, it is.

What does opportunity cost have to do with resolving your tax problem? Well, not only are you spending your time on more valuable tasks, but you are also making Step 1, Organizing your records, and Step 4, Safeguarding against future tax problems, a lot easier on yourself. In my experience, a business owner who is "doing their own books" isn't doing them at all, and we circle back to being disorganized and not knowing how your business is doing financially. Both are not good situations as you work with the IRS to get your tax problem fixed.

THE HAZARDS OF ASKING FOR ADVICE

Asking others for advice is another topic I feel compelled to address. When facing a situation as challenging as an IRS problem, it's natural to seek out advice. While I believe this is a good thing, it also has some pitfalls you need to be aware of. Here are a few of the more common places you might look for help and the dangers to look out for.

The Internet

We all go to the internet when starting our search for help. This is a great resource and can certainly assist in getting you informed. I encourage you to do this! Obtain as much information as you can so you can make knowledgeable decisions regarding your tax problem.

However, as for any other topic under the sun, the internet can also give you misleading information. While the web can provide you with ideas on the different options available to fix your tax problem, it can also create a false assumption that resolving your issues is an easy project. If it were easy, I wouldn't be writing this book.

There are nuances to every case, and just because one person was able to get a certain result and post about it online doesn't mean you will too. The smallest difference in a situation can make a large difference in the outcome. Do your research, get informed, and use this book as a guide to corroborate what you find on the internet.

Your Friends and Family

Not everyone will ask their friends or family for advice on tax problems because they tend to be a bit embarrassed. For those who do ask friends and family for their two cents, I refer you back to the telephone game we discussed in Chapter Seven. "Success stories" get butchered over time as they pass through communication channels, and by the time they get to you, they could be completely false.

Asking friends and family is particularly dangerous because everyone wants to be helpful. Sometimes, people just like to hear themselves talk and relish the opportunity to bestow their "knowledge" on you. I know these people love and care for you, but the basis of their information is likely to be hearsay with very little foundation in truth. Unless they've gone through their own tax problem, I'd tread lightly. Even then, remember what I've said about every situation being unique and requiring a custom approach.

The Internal Revenue Service

The IRS really tries to be helpful when you reach out to them. Sometimes, you'll even talk with an agent who is nice and seems like they know what they are doing. I have news for you. The collection agent has one job: collecting taxes. Do you think the IRS is going to lay out all your options for success, especially if it involves reducing the amount you owe them? C'mon now, wake up.

You're going to have to call the IRS to negotiate a successful resolution; you just need to be respectfully bold when you make requests. The agent you speak with may tell you something can't be done, but don't be discouraged. Use this book as a guide for your requests. If it's in here, it can be done.

Your Tax Preparer

I have a very high respect for all bonified tax preparers. They're out there doing the best they can to help you obey the tax laws. Still, there are situations where these preparers are out of their league when dealing with complex problems. Many CPA firms refer clients to me because of my specialization in tax problem resolution. If you do ask your tax preparer for advice on fixing your own tax problem, please be aware of the following five untruths.

Untruth #1: All attorneys and accountants have experience with the IRS.

Reality: Only a small number of lawyers and accountants have worked directly with the IRS. Some attorneys just prepare documents, and many accountants only prepare tax returns and perform bookkeeping.

Untruth #2: All tax professionals are trained the same.

Reality: Not all tax professionals have the same training. A Certified Tax Resolution Specialist, for example, undergoes comprehensive training and completes continuing education courses specifically dealing with IRS problems. They specialize in a small niche of the tax world: Tax problem resolution.

Untruth #3: Tax professionals listed on the internet are carefully screened for qualifications.

Reality: The internet can be a valuable tool to search for a tax professional; however, it is also a form of advertising media. Sometimes, the only qualification required to be listed is the ability to pay big bucks for an "exclusive listing." Do your research. Find a company with positive reviews or one that other professionals in your industry endorse.

Untruth #4: A tax professional who can guarantee results must be better than one who cannot.

Reality: No legitimate firm can guarantee results. The IRS decides the outcome of your case. It is only by choosing a skilled and experienced Certified Tax Resolution Specialist that you can increase your chances of a positive result.

Untruth #5: The large, national tax resolution firms have an advantage over a local Certified Tax Resolution Specialist.

Reality: National firms have no advantage over small, local firms and often are at a disadvantage. A local Certified Tax Resolution Specialist knows the local economy and is knowledgeable about other issues that may affect taxpayers living in their area.

CHAPTER 9

Clean Up Your Mess

Why was the seafood restaurant being investigated by the IRS?
Because they were suspected of being a
shell company in some fishy business.

A young lady named Rebecca found herself in a little hot water with the IRS after she started her small business and used incoming funds to pay her staff instead of her taxes. She just saw no other way. Sadly, this is a quite common problem for new businesses and is a horrible idea. I would rather see you get creative to find different ways of taking care of your staff instead of shunning your tax obligations. The IRS comes first, no matter what.

Rebecca was about to marry the love of her life, Joshua, and was resolute in her desire to fix her tax issue. Joshua, a respected professional in the community, was a model citizen and timely tax filer. He had all his financial ducks in order and was not about to tie the knot before his bride-to-be had addressed her IRS situation. Smart.

Fortunately, Rebecca was quite organized, had a nice, clean set of books, and was current on all her tax filings. She'd unknowingly completed the first two steps of the OOPS! process before she'd even reached out to my team for support — something that significantly reduced her resolution timeline.

However, patching up the damage that had already been done remained an issue. Rebecca contacted the IRS and attempted to make a deal but fell woefully short. She just didn't have the knowledge to work with the IRS and ended up right back where she started, staring at a big tax bill that was now even larger due to the accumulation of penalties and interest.

Rebecca engaged my team, and we determined that an OIC was not the best option for her. In working with the IRS collections unit, we were able to set up an installment agreement for her with monthly payments that she could afford. Rebecca and Joshua were thrilled to have this IRS mess behind them so they could move forward with the wedding plans.

This story illustrates the importance of *all* steps in the OOPS! process. Just because you're well organized and file your taxes on time doesn't mean you can resolve your tax balance or stay out of future trouble.

The last two steps of the process are just as important as the first two. Let's now go into some more detail regarding these steps.

PATCH UP THE DAMAGE THAT WAS DONE

Once you've organized your finances and tax documents and observed the tax laws necessary to get back in compliance, it's time to move on to dealing with your tax balance. In Chapter Five, I briefly mentioned three resolution strategies: an offer in compromise (OIC), currently not collectible (CNC) status, and an installment agreement. Now, it's time for a deep dive into each of these options.

Offer in Compromise Details

I tell my clients that there are two primary things that determine whether they qualify for an OIC: what you make and what you've got. An offer acceptance is nearly 100 percent financially based, so the first thing to do is gather your financial information.

Oh, wait! You've already done that in OOPS! Step 1, right? Of course, you have. Grab those net income and net worth figures, as well as your total tax balance from all years; then, we'll continue. If you haven't calculated these totals, flip back to Chapter Six and come back when you're done.

There are two forms you'll need to complete to submit an OIC: a Form 656 and a Form 433-A OIC. You can find these forms, along with instructions on how to complete them, on the irs.gov website.

OOPS! Tip: To find any form on the IRS.gov website, go to the search bar in the upper right-hand corner and type in the word "Form" and the number. Make sure to use the most recent version of the form, as the IRS updates these documents regularly!

Read the instructions provided on both documents very carefully! An OIC is a legal agreement between you and the IRS. It is critical that you know what you're getting into! Follow the steps in the instructions exactly as they are listed. The result is an offer package you'll mail to the IRS offer unit.

After you send in your offer, the IRS will process it and validate your eligibility. It will take several months before the IRS looks at your offer, so you need to be patient. Once the offer unit contacts you, they'll review the offer with you, ask some clarifying questions, and likely request additional documentation. The IRS is strict about their OIC guidelines, so you'll need to play by their rules here.

Eventually, the IRS will decide to accept, reject, or return your offer. If the offer is accepted, congratulations! You will be given instructions on how to make the offer payment and any additional steps to complete the process. Bear in mind that after you get an accepted offer, you are on a five-year tax probation (details about this probation are included in the instructions you read on Form 656). During this period, you must file and pay your taxes on time, or the offer will be negated. After all your hard work, that's certainly something you don't want!

If your offer is rejected, you still get another bite at the apple. You can request an appeal of the decision by sending a letter to the IRS office that sent you the rejection letter. You'll need to identify the specific areas where you disagree and provide documents to support the income item, expense item, and/or asset value that you are disputing.

If your offer is returned, it's the end of the road. You'll either need to start over and prepare another offer or investigate the other resolution options included in this book. Do not submit another offer that looks just like the first one that was returned. It's a waste of time, and you'll be sorely disappointed. Only resubmit an offer if your financial condition has significantly changed or if you didn't properly follow the IRS offer guidelines the first time.

Currently Not Collectible Details

To start the process of getting into a currently not collectible status (CNC), go to irs.gov and find Form 433-A. Use your financial information from OOPS! Step 1: Organize to complete the form. If your net income is zero or below and your net worth is zero or below or you have some extenuating circumstances, the CNC might be your best bet. If those numbers are higher than zero, an installment agreement is likely the way to go. I'll give you a full breakdown of installment agreements in the next section.

Once you have Form 433-A filled out, call the IRS at the number on your most recent notice. First, they'll ask you several questions to validate that you are who you say you are. Then, you'll tell the IRS that you are not able to pay the amount due and ask them to put you in a CNC status. The IRS will likely ask you for Form 433-A (which you've already completed) and review it with you. The agent will then decide if you qualify for a CNC (or refer you to a different department that will) and tell you what to do next.

If approved, the IRS will suspend collection action and release any wage and bank levies. If not approved, an installment agreement is the route to take.

Does this sound too good to be true? You just call the IRS, tell them you can't pay, and they leave you alone? Well, it is. Naturally, there are some downsides. First, the IRS isn't forgiving your tax debt; they are just allowing you to delay payment until you can afford to start paying them again. Nuts.

Second, during the time your account is in the CNC status, penalties and interest continue to accrue, making your balance increase on a daily basis. If you do the math, this could really add up.

Third, the IRS will likely take any future tax refunds that you have coming to you. This is a bummer because it's the one time you *like* seeing a letter from the IRS because it contains a check payable to you. No-go.

Finally, the IRS can file a notice of federal tax lien while you are in CNC status. Remember when we talked about liens in Chapter Four? No? I'll remind you: it's not something you want.

The CNC is not a permanent solution; you're just kicking the can down the road. The IRS will review your CNC periodically, and if they deem you can now pay, collection action will resume. While this option is only temporary, it still may be appropriate for your specific situation.

Installment Agreement Details

The last collection alternative is an installment agreement. There are multiple varieties of installment agreements (or payment plans). One of them is a short-term payment plan. If you owe less than $100,000 in taxes, penalties, and interest and can pay in six months or less, you can apply for a short-term payment plan online. Go to irs.gov and type "payment plan" in the IRS search bar. This is the quickest, easiest payment plan and if your balance is low enough, you'll get approved on the spot. You won't even need to provide financial information.

Of course, not everyone can pay their tax balance in six months, which is where the long-term payment plan comes into play. If you owe $50,000 or less ($25,000 or less for a business) in combined tax, penalties, and interest, you can apply for this one online as well. The IRS will usually let you take up to three years to pay your tax liability without an issue.

However, if you don't qualify for online application, or you would rather send your request to the IRS another way, you should complete Form 9465 Installment Agreement Request. Form 9465 and its instructions can be found on irs.gov. With this payment plan, the IRS will usually allow you to pay over a six-year timeframe with a long-term installment agreement.

An advantage of setting up an installment agreement with the IRS is that if you are current on your payments, the IRS will stop its aggressive collection tactics, and you won't be in danger of any bank levies or wage garnishments. Also, once you've made your final payment, any liens will be released, and as long as you stay current with filing and paying your taxes, you won't have to worry about any more IRS problems!

Alrighty, that's OOPS! Step 3: Patch up the damage that was done! Congratulations on making it this far! If you've followed all the steps up to this point, you're more organized than you've ever been, you're in full compliance with the IRS, and you've implemented a final resolution to your tax problem. Pause and consider how you felt about your tax problem when you received that first letter compared to how you feel about it now. What a difference, right? Now, let's maintain this state of mind by completing OOPS! Step 4: Safeguarding against future tax problems.

SAFEGUARDING AGAINST FUTURE TAX PROBLEMS

The first strategy to safeguard against future tax problems pertains to those who are full-time employees. If this is you, look at your most recent paycheck. Is the proper amount being withheld? If you're not sure, go to irs.gov and use the Tax Withholding Estimator I mentioned in Chapter Five. It is your responsibility to tell your employer to withhold the right amount via Form W-4. Remember that form you filled out when you first started with the company? Yep, that's the one — and it's important.

I see employees get tripped up when they experience a significant life event and fail to consider the tax implications. One example is selling your home and downsizing to a condo you rent. There may have been large tax deductions you took advantage of with your house that you no longer have access to.

Another is when your kids grow up and move out on their own. Losing those not-so-little dependents could have a big impact on your taxable income. Not adjusting your withholding to line up with your new life could get you in trouble on April 15th.

There are many scenarios like this that could get you sideways with the IRS. If you experience a life event you suspect could impact your taxable income, use that Tax Withholding Estimator tool on the irs.gov website to see if an adjustment needs to be made to your Form W-4.

If you are self-employed or if you are employed and have a side gig, you must be making estimated tax payments. I've seen so many people mess this up (remember Jim and Beth from Chapter One?). It is imperative that you make estimated tax payments either online at irs.gov or by mailing in a check with a Form 1040-ES Payment Voucher, found on the IRS.gov website. These payments need to be made on a quarterly basis, and each payment you make needs to be designated specifically for the current year.

OOPS! Tip: If you send a payment to the IRS and don't indicate what period the payment is for, they will apply the payment to whatever period is in the best interest of the IRS, which may not be in *your* best interest! For example, you may be thinking that you're making an estimated tax payment for the current year, but if you don't make that clear to the IRS, they could apply it to another year without you even knowing it!

Making payments to the IRS via irs.gov is fine; just verify that you have selected "Estimated tax payment" for the current year in the drop-down box asking you what the payment is for. If you prefer to mail the IRS a check, write your social security number and "Estimated tax payment for [the desired quarter and year]" on the check's memo line. Include a fully completed voucher for that same quarter and year with your payment, and mail it to the IRS address shown on the voucher instructions.

To determine the proper amount owed for your estimated tax payments, use the IRS Form 1040-ES for the current year. There is a worksheet inside the instructions where you can enter the estimated business profit for the year and calculate your quarterly estimated tax payment by walking through the steps.

Finally, make sure you do your bookkeeping! This is imperative when you have your own small business. You need to have a solid understanding of your business profits to determine if you are making the proper estimated tax payments. Please do not overlook this! I know it's a pain and doesn't seem very important, but having a current set of books will not only help you stay up-to-date on your taxes but also give you peace of mind that you won't get surprised at the end of the year when you find out how great your business did — and how much your tax bill is!

When your business grows to any scale, hire a company to prepare your books for you. Yes, I get it. It's another administrative cost that doesn't generate income. However, your superpower is not doing books. It's running your business. Pay someone else to prepare your books and then hold monthly or quarterly meetings with them to review a profit and loss statement and balance sheet with you. Don't just set it and forget it! It's *your* responsibility to oversee the company preparing the set of books.

Having a company prepare your taxes and books will be crucial when you grow your business. They can advise you on how much your estimated tax payments should be, keep you in filing compliance, and help you identify any financial blind spots you may have.

That's it for OOPS! Step 4: Safeguarding against future tax problems! You've organized your records, obeyed the tax laws and gotten into compliance, patched up the damage that was done, and safeguarded against future tax problems. The OOPS! process is complete! Hopefully, you feel like a huge weight has been lifted off your shoulders — because it has!

CHAPTER 10

You Can Do This!

Do not wait to strike till the iron is hot,
but make it hot by striking.
— **WILLIAM BUTLER YEATS**

A HAPPY ENDING

Remember Jim and Beth? Well, we worked through the OOPS! process over the course of a few months, and they were amazing! They responded to my requests with haste, kept a positive attitude, and trusted the process. I only needed to remind them to be patient as these government agencies don't operate quickly or efficiently.

For Jim and Beth, the process from start to finish took about five months. After everything was complete, I made my favorite client phone call to them. Jim had me on speaker. "Ok, guys, the results are in!" I said.

"I'm so nervous. Are we safe? Were you able to save us any money," Beth cautiously responded.

"Yes, and yes!" I happily replied. "We have an approved installment agreement that will save you about $50,000. You are now in full compliance with all tax laws. And because of the controls we put in place over these last few months, you are protected from any future tax problems!"

Silence.

"Hello?" I said.

After a few deafening moments, a sniffling Jim said, "Ben, you saved our financial lives. I don't know how we can possibly repay you."

"Jim, you already did with this phone call!" I said. "Oh, and there's one more thing. I was able to prevent the wage garnishment on Beth's paycheck."

Beth screamed with joy.

YOUR NEW LIFE

What would resolving your tax debt mean in *your* life? How would you feel, act, and behave knowing you could walk out to your mailbox with confidence? When you lay your head down at night to go to sleep, would your face have a smile on it instead of a frown? How would your relationship with your spouse change? What about your kids? Would you have more patience and understanding with them in their everyday lives? How would finally being free from the clutches of the IRS impact your productivity at work or your success with your business?

Seems impossible? It isn't.

Let me tell you how being free from IRS problems affected Kasey, one of my recent clients. Kasey was a partner in a small business with financial troubles that left him with an outstanding IRS balance of $135,000. On top of that, Kasey and his wife Ariel had a newborn boy named Kory, who was born with significant health problems. The stress of the IRS bearing down on Kasey impacted his ability to handle all the challenges that come with nurturing a child who has been diagnosed with permanent physical and mental disorders.

Kasey now had a full-time job, and his dire situation really moved me. I told him I'd shoulder the pressure of the IRS while he focused on his family. Kasey felt immediate relief, and I vowed to fight for the best possible outcome for him.

After our initial analysis, I determined that submitting an OIC would be the best path for Kasey and Ariel. I was confident we had a strong case, but with the IRS, there are no guarantees. Basically, they are the judge, jury, and executioner when it comes to OICs.

I put on my armor (blazer), sharpened my sword (pencil), and started with Step 1 of the OOPS! process: organizing their records. Fortunately, Kasey had saved all his old tax documents and was able to retrieve them quickly. Step 1: check!

Next was to obey the tax laws and get compliant. Step 2 was easy to check off the list because Kasey was current on his tax filings and was having the proper amount of taxes withheld from his paycheck.

I knew Step 3 would be the biggest challenge. We had to get the offer prepared, sent in, negotiated, and finalized. Patching up the damage on this case was going to be tough, but I was up for it!

Financial analysis and supporting documentation reign supreme when it comes to successfully submitting an OIC, so I gathered well over a hundred pages of bank statements, doctor invoices, case studies, insurance policies, and diagnosis notes. It was a heavy lift, but I was re-energized every time I read a doctor's prognosis for Kory. I felt a moral obligation to help Kasey and Ariel. They had their hands full with Kory's health.

I prepared the financial statement Form 433-A OIC and Form 656 with pinpoint accuracy, bundled it together with my supporting documentation in a nice package and mailed it in. Now, it was time to hurry up and wait.

Using my transcript monitoring program, I could see that the offer was received, so I knew it had arrived at the IRS offer unit. Weeks went by. Then months. Still no response from the IRS. I talked to Kasey regularly, assuring him that this was a part of the process and that we just had to be patient.

Finally, one sunny, warm Monday morning, my phone rang. It was the IRS offer unit. I held my breath.

"Mr. Butterfield, this is Ms. Adams with the IRS. We received your offer package, and we have a few questions," she started. I knew all the work I'd completed up to this point had prepared me for this moment. Now, I was in the arena, and it was time for the real battle to begin.

The amount of additional documentation Ms. Adams requested was obscene. I felt like she was asking for an original copy of the Declaration of Independence! Regardless, I had to follow the rules. I was given two weeks to put together another package with responses to the additional request. The new package was dozens of pages long when complete, and I sent it in.

A week went by. Then two. I sent a message to Ms. Adams through the IRS's secure portal asking if she'd received the package. No response. A month went by. I sent another message along with a fax. Still nothing.

This delay was not normal. Usually, when you are assigned an offer agent, they are relatively responsive since their priority is to get cases completed and closed.

Finally, Ms. Adams called me. "I apologize for the delay, Mr. Butterfield, but my computer was down for a month, and I couldn't work on your case."

A month? Are you kidding me? How can a computer be "down" for a month? I thought. *Oh well, at least she's finally called me to continue the process.* I braced myself.

"After my computer got fixed, I had to go through all the documents you sent me. It took three days! You gave me so much!" Ms. Adams complained.

Nothing should surprise me with the IRS, but I was befuddled. "I just gave you everything you asked for, nothing more," I whispered under my breath.

The phone call lasted more than two hours. Ms. Adams was trying to poke holes in every single document. She challenged one thing after another. She sensed my growing frustration, tensions rose, and she said, "I'm sorry, Mr. Butterfield, but I'm afraid we are going to return your offer. You will have no appeal rights, and I will consider the case closed."

It was a sword strike right between my breastplates. I had failed. I understood that not all outcomes were going to be perfect, but this one hurt. An image of little Kory's face entered my consciousness.

Not now. Not today, I thought. I was down but not out. Ms. Adams was abusing her power, and we both knew it. In a calm but stern voice, I told her, "I would like to speak with your manager immediately."

Ms. Adams, taken aback and knowing that I wasn't messing around, responded, "Would you like me to officially file a request for a manager conference?"

"Yes," I replied.

The phone call ended quickly after that. I wasn't about to be bullied, and I certainly wasn't going to give up on Kasey, Ariel, and little Kory. I knew the IRS playbook just as much as, if not more than, Ms. Adams. Her power trip wasn't going to fly with me.

Two hours later — I kid you not, two hours — my phone rang.

"Mr. Butterfield, this is Ms. Adams. I've decided not to return your offer. There are just a few more documents I need from you, and then we can have another discussion." I barely recognized her voice; it was sweet as pie! Go figure. Sometimes, bullies just need to be punched in the nose.

The next round began. I knew this would be a battle, and I was right. I prepared yet another package of documents and sent it to Ms. Adams by the required deadline.

Ms. Adams didn't take very long to respond this time. "Mr. Butterfield, my manager and I have decided to approve your offer as presented."

Bam! Just another day at the office.

This is what I do. I fight vigorously for my clients, and I love it. Many would have given up, but not me. Taxpayers have rights, and sometimes, the IRS needs to be reminded of these rights. Now comes my favorite part.

"Hey, Kasey, this is Ben," I said. "I have good news! The IRS has accepted our offer to settle your $135,000 balance for $10,000."

Kasey's emotions poured through the phone. "Oh, thank God," Kasey responded. "This is amazing! I don't know what to say!"

"Go tell Ariel and give Kory a hug for me," I exclaimed.

Results like the outcome of Kasey's situation do happen, and they can happen for you! The OOPS! process was designed to arm you with the tools necessary to get your financial ducks in a row, resolve your IRS debt, and get you the heck off the IRS radar! Just imagine the feeling of accomplishment when you improve your financial picture in such a meaningful way.

Let me tell you one more story, this time about Gonzalez. Gonzalez contacted me about a very large tax bill the IRS was about to assess him. It was more than $190,000! He owned a small construction business, was a very hard worker, and only spoke broken English. Gonzalez relied heavily on his accountant to handle the situation, but unfortunately, things spiraled a bit, and the IRS was sticking to its guns.

After my first discussion with Gonzalez, I realized two things. First, the IRS was not playing by the rules, and second, a language barrier might be making things difficult between Gonzalez, his accountant, and the IRS agent. I called the IRS agent, faxed her my power of attorney, and got to the bottom of things.

As it turned out, there was a serious lack of succinct documentation and, indeed, a bit of a language barrier. Lucky for me, I had resources to handle the translation, and we were able to clearly communicate both to Gonzalez and then back to the IRS agent.

We gathered and summarized hundreds of pages of supporting documents over the course of the next few weeks. Color coding, making reference marks, providing detailed descriptions — you name it, we did it. I knew we only had one shot at this since the IRS was days away from closing the case and assessing the full $190,000. I wasn't about to leave an ounce of doubt, and I presented our case so clearly that a fifth-grader could follow it.

The IRS agent was so impressed by our final package that she accepted all our receipts and reduced the bill to $56,000 — a savings of more than $134,000! Gonzalez was thrilled when I made my favorite phone call to give him the good news. Even though I had my translator on the call, I didn't need her to tell me he was excited!

In addition, I was able to work with the IRS agent and set up an affordable monthly payment plan for the remaining $56,000 balance. The auditor was happy she was able to close this case (IRS agents are overwhelmed with cases!), Gonzalez was happy we were able to save him so much money, and I was happy I could help!

Here is a little quiz question for you: which OOPS! step would have saved Gonzalez, his accountant, and the IRS auditor months of anguish? Step 1: Organize, of course! If you answered Step 4, you get partial credit. If Gonzalez's records had been organized and airtight, the IRS agent would have been able to understand his business and related expenses more clearly.

NOW WHAT?

How do you eat an elephant? One bite at a time. I always found this reference curious. I mean, does anyone really want to eat an elephant? Is it even legal? Why don't we say tomahawk steak or watermelon instead? Regardless, the metaphor is applicable to how you must be feeling right now: overwhelmed, fearful, and nervous.

I understand. I hear these feelings in the voices of my clients every day. It's okay, you're not alone.

Having said that, it *is* time to take that first bite. Your health, relationships, and financial well-being are counting on it. Most people believe they need to muster up the confidence to take action, but the opposite is actually true. You gain confidence by taking action first. Now that you've read this book, there are no excuses left. Start with OOPS! Step 1: Organize your records.

While I wrote this book to give you the tools and processes needed to resolve your tax problem on your own, sometimes you just have to call in a professional. Every situation is unique since there are so many variables involved, and the IRS, with its incredible power, is constantly an unknown factor. Having a professional who knows the IRS playbook and who will fight for you will tilt the odds of success heavily in your favor.

Most CPAs don't specialize in tax problem resolution. A client with tax problems is a disruption to their flow of business, and they either don't want to or don't know how to deal with it. I do. I'm on the phone with the IRS almost every single day. Tax problem resolution is my specialty.

The OOPS! process has worked and continues to work well for me and the clients I serve. The stories in this book are all real (although the names have been altered), and no matter how dire your specific situation is, I can find a solution to every problem. The life you envision, the life with no IRS letters, calls, or visits to your house, is possible. A life where once-strained relationships are now healed is possible.

We'd be honored to give that life to you. All you have to do is reach out to us for a free initial consultation.

About the Author

BENJAMIN P. BUTTERFIELD is the founder and CEO of BPB Tax Resolutions, one of the nation's leading tax negotiation and mediation firms, which boasts an A+ Better Business Bureau rating. Winner of the Roz Strategies Outstanding Achievement in Tax Resolutions award in 2024 and author of the book *OOPS! The Indispensable Guide to Resolving Your Tax Problem*, Ben has helped hundreds of taxpayers overcome seemingly insurmountable odds with federal and state taxing agencies. Ben is an Enrolled Agent, has an MBA from the University of Nebraska, and holds the coveted Certified Tax Resolution Specialist designation. Father of three and an avid reader, Ben enjoys traveling, the outdoors, playing pickleball, and recently found an interest in performing improv.

CONTACT

🌐   BPBTaxResolutions.com

in   BPB Tax Resolutions

f   BPB Tax Resolutions

📷   BPB Tax Resolutions

DO YOU WANT THE EASY BUTTON?

We highly recommend you let a professional resolve your tax problem. Visit us at BPBTaxResolutions.com or scan the QR code below to set up a free initial consultation.

BPBTaxResolutions.com/Contact-Us